Rescue from Rejection

Finding Security in
God's Loving Acceptance

Denise Cross

Sovereign World

Sovereign World Ltd
PO Box 784
Ellel
Lancaster LA1 9DA
England

www.sovereignworld.com

Unless otherwise stated, all Scripture quotations are taken from the New King James Version (NKJV), copyright © 1983, 1992 by Thomas Nelson, Inc. Scriptures marked GNB are taken from the Good News Bible published by The Bible Societies/Collins © American Bible Society.

HE KNOWS MY NAME/WALKER TOMMY © 1996 Doulos Publishing / Maranatha! Music / Music Services (Admin by Song Solutions CopyCare, 13 Horsted Square, Uckfield, East Sussex, TN22 1QG www.songsolutions.org). Used by permission.

ISBN 978 1 85240 538 0

The publishers aim to produce books which will help to extend and build up the Kingdom of God. We do not necessarily agree with every view expressed by the authors, or with every interpretation of Scripture expressed. We expect readers to make their own judgment in the light of their understanding of God's Word and in an attitude of Christian love and fellowship.

Cover design by ThirteenFour Design
Typeset by documen, www.documen.co.uk
Printed in the United Kingdom

Contents

	Author's Preface	5
	Introduction	7
Chapter 1	Accepted or Rejected – How Do You Feel?	9
Chapter 2	The Beginning of the Problem – Who Rejected Whom?	19
Chapter 3	Life Foundations – How Good Was Your Start?	25
Chapter 4	Family Reality – Is God Really Like This?	40
Chapter 5	The Reality of Life – Will Everyone Reject Me?	58
Chapter 6	Deceptive Lessons from the School of Life – Are You Good Enough to be Accepted?	69
Chapter 7	My Response to Rejection – What Else Could I Do?	80
Chapter 8	Accepting Yourself – Who Makes the Grade?	94
Chapter 9	It Isn't Fair – Who Cares About Me?	104
Chapter 10	The Search for Identity – Who Am I?	113
Chapter 11	The Walk Forward – Will You Choose New Truths or Old?	129
Chapter 12	Sowing and Reaping Acceptance – Anyone for a Lifestyle Change?	143
Appendix	Testimonies of Rescue	148
	About Ellel Ministries	154
	About the Author	156

Author's Preface

We are not strangers to the issue of rejection; first-hand experiences have left their mark on many of us. We live in a world that makes demands on us: demands to be "good enough" to be valuable, or to be worthy to be counted "in." Many who try and fail to meet what seems the required standard for acceptance assume they must be totally unacceptable; those who feel this way might consider themselves as "rejects." Yet others strive for a modicum of acceptance by desperately trying to please those around them.

These past experiences of rejection have also sowed into us beliefs about who deserves to be accepted and loved. These beliefs lead us into judging others, who in turn judge us and often reinforce our beliefs about our own unacceptability. Perhaps the most damaging result of these experiences is that they may have led us to assume that God assesses our worth in the same way – but we have got that absolutely wrong!

The amazing truth is that God's great love for us is not in any way conditional. His love isn't altered by what we do: He is eternally unchanging and constant in His love toward us. However, the cold reality is that despite our best efforts to believe this truth, the doubts can arise, often in wakeful small hours of the night when the sense of our worthlessness crowds in and feelings of rejection overwhelm us. How is it that what we can understand in our head from the written Word can still fail to satisfy the seemingly insatiable hunger for reassurance of God's love and acceptance in our innermost being?

This book is written to help you, the reader, to understand how you might have got "the wrong end of the stick" about God's love and acceptance. My desire is to help you to discover what has affected your ability to live confidently in the fullness of God's amazing truth about you: you are of great value and immeasurable worth to Him and He accepts you unconditionally.

Together we will consider the effect of the rejecting experiences of our lives from the very first moment of our physical existence on earth. We will consider, with the help of the Holy Spirit, how we can learn to recognize and erase the erroneous beliefs which have been laid down as foundations in our heart and on which our lives have been built. We will consider how our desperation for acceptance has led us into sinful lifestyles: sin that now spoils our ability to hear clearly from our Father, and to receive His much-needed comfort into the places of wounding.

What joy it is that we have a Savior, our Redeemer, who will wash us clean from our sin and, if we are willing, write His truth on our hearts: the amazing truth that we are unconditionally accepted and, through Jesus, eternally included in God's family. We belong to Him and can share in an inheritance of all His blessings.

Understanding and appropriating these truths will revolutionize our lives. We will be able to walk in a new freedom as the light of God's glorious acceptance finally dispels the rejection that has thrown a dark, cold shadow over us. All our relationships cannot help but benefit from such a significant change, and whatever arrows of rejection come our way in the future, nothing will be able to steal from us that inner peace that comes from knowing that we are unquestionably cherished and loved, as a child of God.

Introduction

Some years ago I was taking part in an Ellel Ministries teaching conference in Switzerland and on a free afternoon a few of the team took the opportunity to go and see some traditional glass-blowing. The glass-blowers stood around a huge furnace and, working in sweltering heat, were fashioning objects of various shapes and sizes. I was drawn to watching two men who were working together. One was blowing through a long pipe into a lump of molten glass, and the other was holding the emerging green glass vessel in a set of giant calipers. It was clearly going to be something enormous.

Together they worked for many minutes, intermittently putting the glass back into the furnace to keep it soft and pliable, forming an intricate, many-waisted vase. When at last the shaping was finished, they completed the top lip and then the base. Finally, just as they were about to cut the vase off from the remaining molten glass, the "blower" held the huge vase up to the light to inspect it. It looked fabulous to me, but without a second thought he threw the newly finished article down into a huge wooden box beside him and it smashed into a million small pieces. It was not good enough. It was below the standard required. It was rejected.

Many of us feel like that vase. We feel we have been held up to the light and been found to be wanting – substandard and inadequate. We feel smashed by the experiences of life, and can't believe that we'll ever be able to make the grade.

The truth is that unconditional acceptance and a sense of belonging is our inheritance through Jesus Christ our Lord. We are not rejected; we are unconditionally accepted. The enemy has stolen the truth from us for too long. Today is a good day to start claiming back what is rightly ours, not just as head knowledge but as a deep and life-changing assurance in our hearts. Then we will all be able to declare, "I'm accepted. I'm forgiven. I am loved by the True and Living God."

CHAPTER 1

Accepted
or Rejected –
How Do You Feel?

What is rejection?

You can learn a lot by watching children playing in a park. One day I was watching some five-year-olds chasing each other around a grassy area. After some time a little boy who had been sitting on a bench nearby got up to join in the game. As he approached, one of the girls who was involved in the game stopped and, looking him straight in the face, said loud and clear, "Go away – we aren't playing with *you*." Without comment or argument the boy returned forlorn to his bench and the girl went back to her game. He accepted her verdict – he was rejected.

Perhaps the rejection in your life hasn't been expressed as bluntly as that, but rejection has touched most of us. We have known its sting in the past and may still feel its pain regularly from a multitude of small rebuffs. Who among us hasn't been rudely and dismissively treated by over-zealous officials, or even been verbally abused by an irate stranger pushing past us in the street? We live in a world where, daily, people feel the sting of being devalued and rejected. Some have had to endure major rejections that have shaken their world and their sense of acceptance to the core. Like the wife whose husband walked away with a younger, more exciting lover, leaving her alone, abandoned, and devastated after many years of marriage. Or the man who discovered that his so-called best friend had lied about him to a mutual acquaintance, thirty years before, and this had severely impacted his career opportunities. Or the child sent abroad to live with a distant aunt because his new stepfather didn't want to have him around as a reminder of his wife's former relationship.

Rejection comes in many forms. There is rejection that comes from family members, which we may have had to endure through all our early life; rejection from a supposed friend who turns away in our time of need; rejection from workmates who, desiring to be upwardly mobile, drop us in favor of a more advantageous friendship; rejection from a boyfriend or girlfriend who decides to end what we had hoped would blossom into a marriage relationship; rejection by authorities from whom we are seeking help. Perhaps you recognize the pain of past rejections like these. Large or small, acute or chronic, all situations in which we are rejected devalue us in some way, and cumulatively they can smash our fragile sense of our own identity and worth.

The past is now past, but the sting of rejection can and does linger on. That small boy in the playground accepted his fate, but his heart grieved for what he could not have. The pain he suffered was enough to ensure he didn't attempt to join in again. He was afraid of further rejection. He desired acceptance and to be part of the group but he received rejection, and so he accepted his fate and settled for isolation. Sadly, even after many years, our heart may still be grieving for a true sense of acceptance and belonging that seems to elude us. We need to be real, face our places of anguish and fear, and admit that a sense of rejection can still be lingering in the heart of a Christian like you or me.

What is acceptance?

Acceptance is the opposite of rejection. Acceptance means to be adequate, suitable for the task, approved, and wanted. But even acceptance comes in many "hues." To understand these shades of acceptance it might help to think about how we accept a gift.

There's the grey type of acceptance. Think of the way you rather disinterestedly receive the annual Christmas parcel from Great-Aunt Edith, knowing full well it will be knitted bed socks… again! You accept the parcel graciously, write the thank-you note dutifully, but out of good manners rather than out of a delighted excitement at the gift. This present will reside in your drawer until you can discreetly pass it on to the local charity shop. Accepted? Barely!

Then there is the pastel-colored acceptance when you receive a kind and useful present from a loved friend, and try hard to use it and enjoy it! Your thanks are real and warm, but frankly it would never have been your choice and it doesn't match the kitchen colors. The gift will eventually be relegated to the back of the cupboard, unused but retained so as not to hurt the giver. Accepted? Yes, but in an unexcited way.

Contrast these with the Technicolor acceptance of a child receiving their Christmas parcel – "Just what I wanted!" They can't wait to get it out of the fancy paper and they tear open the box (who needs the label or the instructions?). They are ecstatic to have in their grasp, at last, what they have waited so impatiently for. Their ongoing delight is evidenced when they insist on taking it to bed with them. Each day is better for having it, and they delight in using it and just owning it! Accepted? Definitely!

That's real acceptance. And that's how God accepts us – He delights over us with singing.

The LORD your God is with you;

his power gives you victory.
The Lord will take delight in you,
  and in his love he will give you new life.
He will sing and be joyful over you.

(Zephaniah 3:17 GNB)

And He promises never to let anyone snatch us out of His hand
(John 10:29). Every day He revels in His wonderful, unique
creation, which is *you!*

Take a moment to dwell on this fact. Does it cause an inner
voice to shout "Not me! He couldn't feel like that about me!"
Where does this inner voice that contradicts God's indisputable
truth come from? We will investigate this in Chapter 3, but
for now we must just recognize that this inner voice is there,
and own the reality of the conflict. Each one of us needs
to agree that there is a battle to really accept the truth that
He delights in me and totally accepts me! Are you up for the
challenge of changing your old beliefs and grasping hold of this
fabulous truth?

God's acceptance

Before we move on, there is another aspect of acceptance that
we must consider. God accepts us *unconditionally.* That means
no conditions attached – absolutely none! Many people find
that almost impossible to accept. They believe that God loves
only good and obedient people. However, let me quote from
Luke 6:35:

> *But love your enemies, do good, and lend, hoping for nothing in return;*
> *and your reward will be great, and you will be sons of the Most High.*
> *For He is kind to the unthankful and evil.*

(Luke 6:35, *emphasis added*)

To be kind and comfortable with those who have acted against Him, God must love them all the same. His mercy is the same for everyone, however they respond to Him, even though many will not realize this. That means He unconditionally accepts everyone, even those who are "unthankful and evil;" that should cover all of us!

Matthew gives us another slant on God's unconditional acceptance:

> *But I say to you, love your enemies, bless those who curse you, do good to those who hate you, and pray for those who spitefully use you and persecute you, that you may be sons of your Father in heaven; for He makes His sun rise on the evil and on the good, and sends rain on the just and on the unjust.*
>
> (Matthew 5:44–45)

God treats everyone the same – the evil and the good. His nature is to love, and you can't love those you don't accept. He accepts all He has made; He cannot be untrue to His nature.

Paul says to the Romans:

> *But God demonstrates His own love toward us, in that while we were still sinners, Christ died for us.*
>
> (Romans 5:8)

He didn't wait until we were good enough – we never could be! He loved us first, before we even acknowledged Him.

So, why do some of us think that the Scriptures imply that we need to be good to be accepted? What is usually being said is that we can't receive the blessings of His love and acceptance unless we are obedient. It is true of course that when we are obedient to God, we put ourselves in the place of receiving the fullness of His blessings (Romans 6:16). However, it is equally true that nothing we do, even our disobedience, can or will stop God from loving and accepting us. As the line in the well-known hymn "Great is Thy Faithfulness" by T.O. Chisholm reminds us, "Thou changest not, Thy compassions, they fail not." It is the state of *our* heart that causes the obstacle to receiving *His unconditional acceptance.*

Nowhere in the Scriptures is it made clearer than when Jesus – the only One who fully and completely knows the Father – told the Parable of the Prodigal Son. It is a well-known and much-loved Scripture but maybe we miss the main point of the story: the unconditional acceptance of the Father (Luke 15:11–32). The story, if Jesus told it today, might go something like this:

> *There was a man who had two sons. The younger son was something of a challenge to his dad. He was a rebellious young man with "attitude." He was desperate to get away from what seemed like the restrictions of home life, and taste the high life (or was it the low life?). Amazingly, his father not only let him go but, by selling his business, gave the lad money to finance the trip. The plans were made, the designer clothes selected, and the air tickets bought. Without a thank-you or a backward glance the lad was off to find adventure.*
>
> *Possibly people labeled his dad an over-trusting fool and sniggered behind his back at how he had been taken for a ride by the son. But his dad was unperturbed by their gossip; he had only one concern. Daily he went to the airport to watch out for his son returning. He just couldn't keep away. Was it weeks, months, or years? The old man watched constantly while the community laughed, until their mirth gave way to pity.*
>
> *Then one day it happened. There, could he dare to believe his eyes? Coming through the arrivals gate was a young man. The gait was familiar but the person so changed. Gone were the Armani suit and the swaggering walk. Instead he saw a travel-worn, world-weary, drained down-and-out, wearing soiled clothes and a glazed expression of despair. Others seemed to be avoiding contact with the man – he looked unkempt and most unsavory.*

But the dad didn't hesitate. He ran, jumping the barrier, pushing past the loaded trolleys, and taking off his Burberry coat as he went, he threw himself at the bewildered young man and kissed him. What a homecoming! No words were needed; the message was clear from his actions: "You are my son and I am deliriously happy to have you back." The old man's coat was lovingly wrapped over the scarred arms and filthy clothes, and he proudly led his son out into the world, head held high.

That's unconditional acceptance! Do you get the point?

This is our Heavenly Father. He unconditionally accepts us, dirty sin and all, and we don't have to do anything to win His love. We merely need to *accept that it is the truth and receive it*, just as the dumbfounded prodigal son did. Then we can join in the celebrations that the Father delights to organize for us, despite our past. And this amazing unconditional acceptance of the Father will, without doubt, cause each of us that have received such a reunion with our Heavenly Father to desire to be cleaned up, so we can fully enjoy this newfound love relationship. We hear the story and find it so easy to identify ourselves with the young son, but have we really ever personally felt the delight of such a homecoming? Could that really be true for you and me?

Am I missing something?

What followed in the story that Jesus told is equally important for us. The older brother physically dwelt in the security of the father's home, but in the story it becomes obvious from his attitude and subsequent anger that he didn't really enjoy a true knowledge of his father's loving heart. He was resentful of his father's gracious treatment of his younger brother. He felt that his work, and therefore he himself, had been overlooked, taken for granted, and undervalued.

In his sense of rejection, he seems to have thought, "Why should this waster, who is so unworthy, receive more than I have ever received?" It is clear that the father loved his sons equally. He had sold all that he had and given the proceeds as an inheritance to them both: the elder son had also been a beneficiary of the handout. However, he had not received this as a love gift but as his dues. His perception was that he had earned it by his daily dutiful labor. It didn't seem to have occurred to him that the basis for his dad's relationship with him was not a business agreement, like an employer buying a service, but was that of a caring father offering him the opportunity to share in each day's tasks.

This older son had made his own decision about the father's motives and had totally missed the truth of his heart. He had believed their relationship to be a type of business arrangement, with an unspoken contract, exchanging his service and duty in return for appropriate financial gain. His motive for working, as he had labored each day, became clear as he spoke. He worked to get something in return. He was obedient because it was expedient to be so, but when someone else, a profligate, was given more than him, he took offense and felt rejected. The truth was he had always missed something of his father's true heart. His understanding was that "you get what you deserve" and he felt he deserved a lot! He had assumed his understanding was the truth, but his "truth" was far from correct; in fact it was not truth at all. He had assumed that he knew his dad's character and motives, but he was completely wrong.

What he had failed to understand was that being obedient for the wrong motive had stolen from him the true sense of being accepted simply for who he was – a precious son. His erroneous belief that love must be earned was the motive for his obedience, and that was his problem. In his striving he became both resentful and grudging.

Motive is important

How many of us serve God in this way? Are we trying to win acceptance through our obedience and self-effort, instead of allowing His unconditional acceptance and grace to touch our hearts with His love? Accepting, receiving, and knowing deep down inside that He unconditionally loves us would stir us to enthusiastic delight in obedience, to show our love response to Him. We would no longer be laboring out of grudging duty or legalism – what a freedom!

There is one more thing for us to consider from this story. The last thing the elder brother wanted to do was accept back his wastrel of a brother, even if his father chose to do so. He judged him to be unworthy of acceptance and possibly felt him no longer worthy to be included in the family. Let's admit it, we feel like the elder brother sometimes. We need to face that unpleasant fact about ourselves. We don't necessarily like accepting all those whom our Father accepts. We see ourselves as more acceptable than some, even if less acceptable than others.

Many people, doubting their own acceptability, strive to earn value and acceptance – to prove they are "good enough" to be accepted. They may seek acclaim through academic study, degrees, and qualifications. They may set themselves ever-higher goals in sports, or devote their every waking hour to winning accolades in business. But success in the world's eyes will never be truly satisfying. Some people try to tread down rivals with criticism or judgment in order to feel more significant themselves. Sadly, these are not only attitudes and behaviors of the unsaved; they can and do affect believers as well.

Change is possible

If we really want to change our attitudes, perhaps we should start now. We need to recognize how our faulty reasoning has developed in us mindsets which are not godly. We have used judgment of others as a form of self-comfort, trying to make ourselves feel more acceptable by judging them less acceptable. But this only serves to increase our own sense of alienation and isolation. We may also have reasoned, erroneously, that God cannot accept us just as we are, since we do not accept others that way.

Our prayer should be that we would allow God to teach our hearts His truth, so we will no longer hold onto our own judgments about others or even about Him. Then we can be free to accept others and, in turn, be accepted by them. We can accept our Heavenly Father as He truly is and, released from "slaving" for acceptance like the resentful older brother in the story, we could allow Him to lovingly embrace us just as we are.

Can we dare to believe the truth that if we never did another good deed and were even prodigal in our living, He would still love us the same? Of course, we would miss out on many blessings which come with obedience, and would reap instead the consequences of our own sin, but He would still love us the same. His heart would grieve for us, but His love and unconditional acceptance would always endure. We cannot earn His love; we cannot stop His love. It is eternal and free!

Why do we struggle so much with believing these truths of God's unconditional acceptance of us? The origin of this problem lies in the Fall, where all our problems began. In the next chapter we will look at what we can learn about the start of the heart-damaging disease of rejection, and how and why this is now a worldwide pandemic.

CHAPTER 2

The Beginning of the Problem – Who Rejected Whom?

Understanding the Fall

So, what happened in that eternity-changing moment of the Fall: that moment that stole our security and robbed us of our confident knowledge that we belonged to God's family? That moment when instead of the delight of unconditional acceptance, rejection was first released into the world? How did the Fall give birth to the atmosphere in which the virus of rejection could infect all of humankind?

The garden scene and fateful action of the Fall are well known: Adam and Eve listened to the voice of the serpent, Satan the enemy of God, and made their choice to eat from the tree of the knowledge of good and evil (Genesis 3:6). They were tempted. That is true. But they themselves used their freewill choice to disobey God, although He had specifically warned them against doing this (Genesis 2:17). Eating this "knowledge" fruit seemed as if it would be so helpful (surely knowledge is always good, isn't it?), but the fruit brought an unexpected bitter aftertaste.

Their action demonstrates the first instance of rejection here on earth – *they rejected God*. They rejected Him by rejecting His instruction and command. But their action had extremely

far-reaching consequences. In that moment a change of spiritual
authority took place. No longer was mankind submitted to God,
an unconditionally accepting and loving Heavenly Father, but
now the whole human race was submitted to that being whom
they had obeyed, namely, Satan (Romans 6:16; 1 John 5:19).

Now, Satan himself had rejected God's sovereignty, wanting
to be like God, which is why his name was changed from Lucifer
to Satan (Isaiah 14:12–14). He is now the adversary of God. He
fell from heaven (Luke 10:18; Revelation 12:9) – since nothing
and no one that will not bow the knee to God can remain in
heaven. Satan thus brought upon himself eternal rejection.
Rejection is part of his character, and those living under his
fathering (John 8:44) will be infected with his traits. Rejection
hurts and wounds people and destroys relationships. It is one of
Satan's best weapons of destruction.

Before the Fall, God knew and unconditionally accepted
Adam and Eve, and they were secure in His love and protection.
They also had a completely "open" relationship between
themselves. The Bible says they were naked but were not
ashamed (Genesis 2:25), which is a physical demonstration of
a spiritual truth – there was nothing hidden between them and
they felt very secure and accepted, even in their nakedness.
Perhaps we can picture these relationships of acceptance
as a triangle. The arrows on the lines denote the flow of
unconditional acceptance.

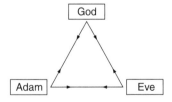

At the Fall, Eve chose to act rebelliously and independently from
Adam, thus breaking the fully open and united relationship
they had previously enjoyed. We could say she rejected Adam,
turned her back on him, and in doing so she put up a barrier

to receiving his acceptance of her. By their joint disobedience, both Adam and Eve broke their open, accepting relationship with God. They rejected God, and they put up barriers to His freely flowing unconditional acceptance. The double lines in the next diagram demonstrate these barriers to God's acceptance, and also Eve's barrier to Adam's acceptance.

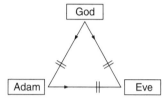

But God is unchanging. He is always unconditionally accepting of His people.

When He tried to reach out in love to Adam, to give him a chance for an open relationship again, Adam refused to be found (he was hiding behind a bush) and, instead of coming to God in humility, tried to defend himself and pointed his finger at Eve. He rejected her by blaming her, and put up a barrier in his relationship with her. Instead of unconditional acceptance, we see the development of a relationship of blame and rejection in an attempt at self-protection. Adam and Eve put up defensive barriers which, in reality, isolate them from each other. The nature of fallen man, which we call "carnality," begins to show. Both Adam and Eve, working out of their carnal natures, display their new inner belief: "I know what is best for me."

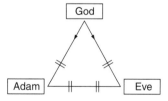

But Adam didn't know what was best for him. He felt rejected and alone. This was because *he* had rejected God and Eve. Eve felt the same: isolated and rejected. And, to make matters worse, they both thought (using the "I know best" thinking of their fallen nature) that rejecting others and protecting themselves might improve their feeling of security. They wanted to feel accepted and secure again because that was what they were created to need, and the assurance of being accepted and the security that flows from it were essential for their spiritual nourishment. But they had no way back to the security of loving and accepting relationships. They were alone and lost.

Is there any hope of rescue?

How could those barriers to the flow of God's acceptance be taken down? God hadn't changed, but somehow they didn't know and couldn't feel His unchanging love and delight in them anymore. They had lost that wonderful and life-giving assurance of unconditional acceptance. Rejection had infected them, and their once-perfect relationship was now severely strained.

What was needed was an exchange, a return to the warmth of acceptance in place of the pain of rejection, and a reinstatement of the open relationship with God which would bring back true security. A renewed potential for living in relationships of unconditional acceptance might then be possible. Thank God that He had already planned for our salvation, and immediately after the Fall He speaks of His wonderful plan (Genesis 3:15).

Jesus was the answer. Isn't He always? At the cross Jesus came to make that way back to God. There is no other way. The cross is the place of divine exchange, to which you can bring your hurting past and dysfunctional present, and go away with something totally different for your future. It is at Calvary that the total rejection brought upon themselves by all of mankind is laid on Jesus, as He shouts out, "My God, My God, why have You forsaken Me?" (Matthew 27:46). The sound must have been unbearable to the Father, but it had to be like that. Jesus had to go through the darkness and despair of that dreadful separation for you and for me. Jesus took the total sin of mankind's rejection of God, to win us back the fullness of acceptance. Jesus took the total sin of all our rejection of each other, so that we might choose a lifestyle of acceptance. Jesus felt the total pain of all our wounds of rejection, so that we might receive comfort and healing. Yes, Jesus is the answer.

When we consider what Jesus has done for us, the despair we have felt because of our own past rejection seems less overwhelming. Because of Jesus and His resurrection from the dead, we now have the possibility to exchange our pain of rejection for His healing, restorative comfort, and unconditional acceptance. The antidote to rejection has been made available, free to all who recognize they need it and are willing to receive it. What a wonderful deal! Who would want to miss the fullness of this amazing, life-changing special offer?

I'd like to make one last point before we move on. It might seem, at first reading, that God did in some way reject Adam and Eve after they had sinned, because He put them out of the Garden of Eden (Genesis 3:23). But, in actual fact, this verse demonstrates God's great love for mankind. His action ensured that they would not eat of the tree of life that was growing in the garden (Genesis 3:22). If they had, they would have lived forever in their unhappy fallen and rejection-contaminated state. It is interesting to note that this verse is an unfinished sentence. God's completion of this sentence, which explains His action, is demonstrated throughout the rest of the Bible. God's answer to the problem of the Fall, including the sense of rejection that every fallen human is born into, unfolds as we read on. During our earthly physical life, we can choose Jesus as our Savior. In our earthly physical death we will eventually be totally and utterly released from our fallen nature and every trace of the rejection that the Fall brought.

The truths of Genesis outline the start of the generic problem of rejection for all of mankind. But, you may be thinking, what about me and my life? Why do I still feel a sense of rejection even though I have accepted Jesus as my Savior? To discover the roots of our own particular issues of rejection we must look back to our own beginning... to day one of our existence, for that is where our own special mix of rejection started.

CHAPTER 3

Life Foundations – How Good Was Your Start?

God's plan was for good

God's perfect plan for you and me was that we would feel secure in His unconditional acceptance right from the very start of our lives. From the moment of our conception we should have been wrapped in the atmosphere of unconditional love, in which we could find security and have the freedom to grow. But, in this fallen world, things are not as God would want them to be. What we need to consider is how it should have been, if it had all been perfect as God intended, and how it actually was!

When God commanded Adam and Eve to multiply (Genesis 1:28), He had envisioned a wonderful plan. Through procreation they would model His creativity and through parenting they would demonstrate His loving Father-heart.

In fact, God's plan was that the parents would welcome and unconditionally accept the child even before he or she was conceived. What a wonderful start – a new little person made by love, through love, to be loved.

Welcomed and accepted

In Luke chapter 1 we read how the angel Gabriel brought
the message from God to Mary saying that she had been
chosen to become pregnant with God's miracle child, His Son
(Luke 1:35–38, 46–49). Before the child was conceived, she was
being asked if she was willing to receive Him, not only physically,
but also if she was ready to open her heart to Him. God was
asking if she would fully and unconditionally accept this child,
whatever the personal cost (Luke 1:38; 2:35). Her openness to
this extraordinary suggestion, and her loving acceptance of this
yet unformed child, were an essential part of God's plan. Her
heart needed to match God's own heart of love. She needed to
acknowledge and affirm this new life, and her unconditional
acceptance was crucial to the nurture of the planned Messiah.

God often uses physical pictures to help us to understand
a deep spiritual truth. Physically, for a baby to develop, the
woman's womb needs to be prepared. The womb lining needs
to be enlarged to receive the little embryo, and this facilitates
further growth and development. Without this preparation the
baby will not be able to grow. In the same way, God's perfect
plan is for the spiritual atmosphere to be prepared to enable
spiritual development. He desires this for every baby. Often, in
the Scripture, God tells prospective parents that they will have
a child, before conception takes place. He wants, not just their
bodies, but also their hearts prepared for the nurture of this
new life. This heart preparation is particularly obvious when
the parents had previously been considered barren. Think of
Samson, Isaac, and John the Baptist as examples.

But how is an underdeveloped and immature baby able to
sense the atmosphere of parental love and acceptance even in
the first days of life? The Bible tells us that each child that is
conceived has a human spirit. Each human spirit is unique to
the person and comes from God, returning to God when the
person dies.

... the LORD, who stretches out the heavens, lays the foundation of the earth, and forms the spirit of man within him.

(Zechariah 12:1)

Then the dust will return to the earth as it was,
And the spirit will return to God who gave it.

(Ecclesiastes 12:7)

The human spirit is the eternal part of each human being and contains their true, God-given identity. The human spirit of the person sustains the whole life of the person.

Each one of us started life as a single cell; I did and you did. Consider who you were in that first moment of your existence. You had only a very small body (you were a microscopic one-cell being), you had no brain to think great thoughts (the brain doesn't begin to develop until week two), but your human spirit was present within you. We can be sure that your human spirit is present from this first moment of life because the first cell must be alive in order to divide to form two cells. That is how life starts.

For as the body without the spirit is dead, so faith without works is dead also.

(James 2:26)

The reality of life

But God's perfect plan was spoilt by man. We live in a post-Fall world, a world that is much less than perfect, and in which rejection is endemic. When we consider our own conception we must face the fact that our biological mum and dad, however good they were, were fallen human beings and were less than perfect. None of us should have any desire to condemn our parents. They, for the most part, did the best they could, but their ability to give us those vital and necessary ingredients of unconditional acceptance, affirmation, and unselfish love from the very start of our lives was limited.

They were wounded people, affected by their own pain of rejection and the hurts from their past lives. They were, as we all are, carnal people, who were to some extent self-focused and quite likely to be totally oblivious of their unborn baby's needs.

The spiritual atmosphere at the time of conception is very important. This moment is one of the most spiritually significant in the whole of life. In that moment the new little life is surrounded with either the goodness of acceptance and belonging, or the toxicity of unacceptability and rejection. Probably for most of us the reality is somewhere between the two extremes. However, the facts are that today many babies are not planned and conceived in a moment of loving marital intimacy, as God had intended. Sadly, too many little ones are brought into being as an unwanted consequence of a lustful, self-gratifying sexual act. Their start in life is tainted with rejection.

However, it is not only those who know that their conception took place outside of a marriage covenant who suffer from these early wounds of rejection. Even within marriage there are children conceived unintentionally or considered to be a "mistake." There are, of course, very many reasons why a child may not be welcomed by his or her parents. For instance, I once ministered to a lady who knew that she was conceived because her mother had conveniently "forgotten" to take her contraceptive pills, when her father was very resistant to the idea of them having a baby. There are also situations where the child is the result of sexual intercourse which, whilst being part of a marriage relationship, was not a union of love but was forced or demanded as a conjugal right. These situations mean the child will have little or no assurance of acceptance by one or both parents, and will feel something of the sting of rejection. Perhaps the most damaging situation for a child is to be conceived as a result of a rape. The violation of the mother, her understandable revulsion at the consequences of the abuse, together with the brutality of the biological father, who has no regard or care for his child, can leave lasting scars of rejection and abandonment on the child.

Why was I conceived?

Even for a child conceived within marriage it may be useful to consider, a little more deeply, exactly why the parents decided to have this child. The reason for this is that the motive for doing something affects the spiritual atmosphere of the action. Actions that may appear on the surface to be good can, on closer inspection, be found to be not quite as they seem. Instead of being motivated by love they may be motivated by selfishness, duty, or conformity. The same action may result in a very different spiritual atmosphere. Jesus knew people's motives because they are spiritually discerned, and He often revealed that He understood them better than the people did themselves. With this in mind we might think to ask ourselves, "Why did my parents conceive me?" The reality is that we cannot be sure, but there may be some clues in our understanding of our history or in the known facts of our early lives.

The issue of parental motives may reveal keys to why some adults feel a deep sense of rejection even though their childhood seems to them to have been normal and accepting for the most part.

It is not unknown for a child to be conceived specifically because of pressure to produce an heir to carry on the family name. I remember one man in Scotland who knew that this was true for him. His mother, when very newly married, had been pressurized by her mother-in-law to immediately have a son to be the next clan chief. But the child could equally well be conceived so he or she can eventually work the family farm, run the family business, or be available to look after the parents in their old age. These children are spiritually affected by the motive of their parents, and can suffer from a lack of acknowledgment for them as individuals. They receive the message that they are a necessary object for the fulfillment of their parents' plans and purposes. But they feel a lack of acceptance, even a measure of rejection, toward them as a unique human being, which may well be exacerbated if they fail to fulfill the parents' planned goal.

Occasionally, a baby is conceived to be a replacement child for one that has died. Sometimes he or she is even given the same name, or a gender-appropriate version of it. These children feel a deep sense of being unimportant simply for who they are, and often grow up with little self-worth. They may even bear a sense of responsibility to keep everyone happy – by being healthy, compliant, and good – but in this they feel as if they are being used and not really personally appreciated. This, unfortunately, can breed deep resentments, and rebellion can follow.

Was I a mistake?

Many adults know they have been carrying a label, "Mistake," all their lives. Their parents may have been unmarried or perhaps they just didn't want a baby at the time of the person's conception. They may have decided it was too soon to have a child, that they had too many children already, or felt that their financial situation was too unstable to afford the expense of a little one. There are many such reasons for parents to feel that this child, at this time, is a mistake. Unfortunately, even if they later love and care for the child, as most do, the lack of the assurance of welcome at conception and in the early days of the unborn child's life is very damaging to the baby's human spirit. The uncertainty the child feels in his spirit leaves him unconnected and without the strong bond of accepting love. He remains spiritually unfed, without the acknowledgment and affirmation intended by God, and lacks the nourishment of acceptance in his innermost being.

We also need to consider the very painful matter of possible attempted abortion. Although historically abortions were illegal, there have always been those who were ready, with various methods, to "help" women to dispose of their unwanted pregnancies. Today, as a legal possibility, many unprepared or unwilling parents can and do consider the option of an abortion during the early weeks of an unplanned pregnancy. But, while the parents consider whether to terminate the life of the baby, the unborn child is living with the imminent possibility of his murder. The baby does not understand this intellectually, of course, but his human spirit senses the very real threat to his existence. There is no greater rejection than to sense that those on whom your life depends are considering rejecting your very existence.

Spiritual nurture is needed

Contrast all these situations with God's perfect plan. His plan was that one man and one woman who loved each other deeply would, through their intimate love, make a new life: procreation to model His creation. God's plan was that all the significant people in a child's early life would reflect something of His faithful, everlasting, unconditional acceptance. His loving character would be practically expressed to each little child from the moment of their conception and reinforced in their life through daily contacts. His love for each one, and His delight in them as an individual, would be laid down in the core of their being and reinforced through the words, attitudes, and actions of those all around them. In a million practical ways His absolute truth would be deposited and reinforced in the child's innermost being, forming a secure foundation, like concrete footings laid down ready to support a beautiful new building.

Since a baby developing in the womb needs physical food in order to grow strong and mature in his body, it is reasonable to expect that he also needs spiritual food to strengthen and feed his human spirit. God's perfect plan was that the human spirit of each developing child would be continually nurtured with unconditional acceptance. His parents, jointly, would acknowledge and affirm the unique and precious life growing in the mother's womb. Their love and affirmation would bring a sense of security and well-being to the developing child, who would flourish in body and spirit. Their unconditional acceptance would give an atmosphere of freedom for the child to grow in his God-given identity.

Parents may be correct in their assertion that *they* didn't plan this child, and perhaps they were very unhappy that the child was developing, but God tells us that no one is a mistake in His eyes. He formed everyone and knew them from before time began.

> *Before I formed you in the womb I knew you ...*
>
> (Jeremiah 1:5)

> *... just as He chose us in Him before the foundation of the world ...*
>
> (Ephesians 1:4)

Acknowledgment is vital

I was teaching one day on these issues and a lady came to me to say that she had always felt she wasn't significant or valuable, and that she felt insecure about her acceptability. We talked about several of the issues of her conception and early days. She told me that her parents were very caring, godly people, and that she was a very much wanted and loved child. She added that she was an only child and treasured by her parents. It seemed that there was no obvious problem in her roots. But God prompted me to ask her how her parents discovered that they were expecting a child. She laughed and told me the story:

They didn't know until my mum was thirty weeks pregnant. They had been told they couldn't have children and had gone to God for comfort in their grief, accepting that this was His will for them, even though they had very much wanted children when they married. It was when Mum was forty that I was conceived. She had thought she was going through the menopause and didn't consider any other reason for the change in her menstruation. When she went to the doctor to help her with her unexplained weight gain they were all totally surprised to discover that she was pregnant. They were, of course, delighted, and a few weeks later I was born.

How could there be this deep sense of insecurity for a much-wanted child like this? The answer lay in the weeks that the child lay in the womb unacknowledged and unaffirmed. It was no one's fault, but it was not what God planned for the feeding and nurture of this little life. She had been starving for love, and it was not knowingly withheld but unknowingly missing. We prayed into this situation, and God spoke right into her human spirit, putting in the words of His assurance of seeing her, knowing her, and loving her from the first moment of her life. She was not alone and unrecognized, but He had seen her. This truth touched her heart deeply and for the first time she could say with certainty:

... You covered me in my mother's womb.
I will praise You, for I am fearfully and wonderfully made;
Marvelous are Your works,
And that my soul knows very well.

(Psalm 139:13–14)

This verse, which she already knew from the Scriptures, became specifically and personally "alive" for her. It is what might be called a *rhema* word: a word that on a specific occasion seems to have a fresh dynamic meaning and often brings significant healing. These words revolutionized her feelings of security and took away the nagging sense of insignificance that had been formed by the circumstances of the earliest part of her life. God restored what had been missing because of the early lack of anchoring to a spiritual love source. He rooted her in His nurturing love. Many of us need these special *rhema* words that God will speak into our lives to bring healing into our innermost being.

Many people who suffer from a lack of the assurance of acceptance are carrying these deep, unexplained feelings that seem to be sown into the very core of their being. They fear that these deep feelings are part of them and always will be. These are very deep roots of rejection in our lives but are by no means the only roots we need to consider.

Before we move on from these earliest moments, we need to think about one other major factor that affects each child as soon as he or she is conceived. The issue is generational inheritance.

Generational inheritance has affected me

We understand this principle of inheritance for the physical body. If parents or grandparents have some physical characteristic or disorder, it is not uncommon for this to be repeated in a child or in future generations. The distortion is carried in the DNA of the parent. For instance, a parent who has a squint affecting his eye would not be surprised if his child had the same problem. The distortion and subsequent dysfunction of the muscles around the eye is passed on to the next generation. Happily, we inherit mostly a body that works correctly as it should, but we may also inherit one or more parts that are in some way not quite right. However we are made, not only body but also spirit, so, in the same way, we also have a spiritual inheritance. The Scripture says we are all affected by the sins of our family line, which gives us an inheritance of iniquity or distortion:

> *Our fathers sinned and are no more,*
> *But we bear their iniquities.*
>
> (Lamentations 5:7)

> *... visiting the iniquity of the fathers upon the children to the third and fourth generations of those who hate Me, but showing mercy to thousands, to those who love Me and keep My commandments.*
>
> (Exodus 20:5–6)

God's plan was for godly parents to send blessings down, as a spiritual inheritance to us, through their righteous living. This would be a sort of spiritual DNA bringing a healthy spiritual life source, forming us and growing us as God intended, with a minimum of distortion. Carnality, however, the distortion of all fallen mankind, is of course present in every human being and sends willfulness and selfishness down to every generation since Adam (Romans 5:12).

We are heirs to the spiritual "right-ness" or "straightness" of our parents, or we can receive something of their spiritual "distortion" or "bent-ness." This spiritual "bent-ness" is caused by their sin and it leaves us with an inheritance which, just like the squint, may cause us very real problems. We need to consider the effect of this spiritual inheritance in the issue of rejection.

So, you may ask, what sin is there in my family line concerning rejection that might affect me? We should consider first: what is sin? Sin is not only what we do. Our beliefs and attitudes can also be sin if they don't agree with God. If the family has developed and nurtured erroneous thinking and understanding about acceptance, for instance that "you can only be accepted if you are good enough to deserve it" or "no one in this family will ever be acceptable," these are sinful statements. With a healthy spiritual inheritance from our parents of right beliefs about God's love and unconditional acceptance, we are better able to form right attitudes towards God and towards ourselves. We are also more capable of truly loving and accepting others. With a distorted inheritance of lies concerning the issues of acceptance, we are much more likely to sin in the same way, because these erroneous beliefs will seem to be truth to us. We have been predisposed by an unrighteous spiritual inheritance.

Consider a person who has an expectation of rejection, inherited through his family line. This will make it more likely that he will see all relationships through "glasses" of mistrust and suspicion, and this will inevitably distort the truth. His expectations may lead him to reject others before they reject him. He may even reject God, and lock himself into a hopeless situation of permanent rejection. His spiritual inheritance is acting like a blindfold that veils the truth about his acceptability. So, from the moment of conception, this lack of ability to receive acceptance through relationships will affect the development of his true identity, and will steal the truth of God's unconditional acceptance.

Perhaps this is most clearly evident when we consider a whole culture that has been rejected. Such a people group may have accepted rejection as a significant feature of their identity. Many black Americans can trace their family line back to those who were bought and sold as slaves. Slaves were deemed less than human and considered to be nothing more than commodities. This deep rejection of their humanity, individuality, and personal worth caused an ongoing generational scar of rejection that can still be detected, outworking in the lives of some people of African descent to this day.

The growth of rejection

Every day whilst a baby is growing in the womb, he is absorbing what is, for the little one, the truth of his existence. It is not necessarily the truth that God wants him to know, but it is the experiential "truth" of his situation. It is in these days that many of the seeds of rejection are sown.

In many families there is a desire for the baby to be of one specific gender. This isn't just a historical problem of Henry VIII and his wives! Perhaps there are already several boys in the family, and a little girl is what everyone would very much like, to complete the perfect family picture. Or maybe there is a desire for Dad to have a son so he can teach him football or fishing. Not being the gender that their parents wanted causes many children to consider themselves as a disappointment. From the first moment of conception the child's human spirit is aware of his or her sexuality. This is an integral part of humanity and is set in the pattern of the chromosomes of a child from their first cell. God's plan for sexuality is clearly that there should be male and female, and that the body should demonstrate the sexuality that God has designated and planned (Genesis 1:27).

However, the desires of the parents for a child of one specific gender can leave the child with a real confusion. Their God-given instinct to please their parents, together with their certainty of their sexuality, may leave them feeling they are intrinsically wrong. There is a deep sense that they will never be able to be what is wanted, and therefore they will never be acceptable. They deem themselves unacceptable by virtue of something that it is impossible for them to change. This deep sense of being unwanted for who they are can be very deeply damaging to a child. Such a deep hurt can even be the starting point of later gender confusion, especially if other circumstances bring similar conflicting messages about the person's sexuality.

One lady recently told me that she hated been fat "like a whale" when she was expecting her child, and had often felt

very angry toward the growing baby who caused her to feel
like that. She wanted to have a baby in her arms but hated the
pregnancy and what it was doing to her body. She had suffered
for years with an eating disorder, and although she was now
much improved, she hated being anything larger than her
normal size 10. When she spoke to me, her little girl, by then
about eighteen months old, was beginning to show some very
distinct signs of insecurity. She had developed severe issues with
eating and was displaying behavior that seemed to be rooted in
a fear of rejection and a need to try to earn acceptance. Her
parents were at a loss to know why she felt so insecure when
she had been so much wanted by them both after several years
of marriage. However, during prayer, God showed her mother
that the resentment she had felt towards her baby in the womb
had affected her daughter. It became clear that this was the start
of the little girl's problems of insecurity; she had felt unaccepted
and unwelcome. Together, Mother and Father were able to
bring this issue before God, and after the mother repented for
her wrong attitude, they were able to ask God to bring healing
and restoration to their daughter. The child was not present,
but their prayer caused a radical change in the child's behavior
from that time forward.

All or any of these issues constitute a lack of unconditional
acceptance, and allow the growth of feelings of rejection, which
steal inner confidence. They occur so early on in our lives,
during our gestation months, that we may assume they are
insignificant. However, they are not unimportant, and looking
at these issues can be a vital part of the healing process.

Safe and secure?

To be safe in the womb of a loving and accepting mother and
secure in the knowledge of the covering of a loving father –
that was the perfect plan. That would have given each of us

the start God intended. But we have seen that it is not always like this, and it may not have been like that for you. It might be helpful to consider what the spiritual atmosphere was like for you personally, in the first nine months of your existence. We may have some relevant knowledge about this time, but we can also ask the Holy Spirit to reveal to us whatever else we might need to know. You may want to make some notes about your own particular situation. Later, in Chapter 11, there are some possible prayers which can help you to pray about these issues. Among them is a prayer about forgiveness, because you will almost certainly need to forgive those who, through their own inability or sin, caused your life to be grounded in rejection rather than in unconditional acceptance.

But unfortunately the bad news is not over yet. Our lives continue to be affected by rejection and we need to be real about how this has happened. If it was in the womb that seeds of rejection were first sown, then the next years are often the years of watering those seeds. What happened in your early years? What messages, spoken and unspoken, did you receive every day of your life about your acceptability? In the next chapter we will consider how these life experiences lay down the distorted feelings we have about ourselves which we know do not agree with God's truth.

It may seem a bit depressing, but facing these issues with reality will start to bring them into the light, where we can invite Jesus, our Healer, into each area of our life that has been darkened by rejection. He is the good news. He is the antidote to all the bad news we may have to face. He can and will "restore the years that the swarming locust has eaten" (Joel 2:25) so we can face whatever difficult truths we need to face, with His hope in our heart.

CHAPTER 4

Family Reality –
Is God Really
Like This?

Happy birth day?

What an amazing thing it is to witness the birth of a new baby! It seems like a miracle when this little wrinkled shape lets out his first yell for the world to hear. It says, "I have arrived – here I am!" For many mothers and fathers this moment releases a surge of maternal and paternal feelings, and in an instant their child is the "apple of their eye," perfectly wonderful and absolutely loved. As one new parent put it recently, "Who could have known that every sneeze, sigh, and blink would be so utterly adorable?" God knew. He planned it to be so (Proverbs 4:3).

I remember this feeling, albeit through a haze of exhaustion, when my own children were born, even though it is now many years ago. In more recent days, in my new role as a grandmother, I have literally been overwhelmed with joy and moved to tears at the excitement of the first meeting with a new and precious grandchild, still wrinkled and blotchy and only a few hours old.

The enormous love and the desire to bond with this new little person leads a mother to want to hold her baby close to her and to feed him at the breast. This is God's plan for the next stage of the child's nurture in both body and spirit. The milk from the mother's breast feeds the body; and the love, physical touch, and joyful smiles from Mum and Dad (even if Baby can't yet focus on them) all feed the spirit with a sense of well-being, acceptance, and security. The child's inner needs are being fed when he is bathed in the atmosphere of his parents' delight in him just because he is who he is. This parental joy is intended to demonstrate an even greater truth, an eternal truth: God Himself rejoices over this little life with singing!

> *The* LORD *will take delight in you,*
> *and in his love he will give you new life.*
> *He will sing and be joyful over you.*
>
> (Zephaniah 3:17 GNB)

The child will continue to learn, over the coming months, about the character of God. Irrespective of whether the parents know and understand this, it will be so. God planned it like this. He planned that, as the relationship with his parents developed, a child would see a reflection of God's love for him, in all its many facets.

What a risk to take! What a responsibility for parents. God trusts this precious little one, whom He loves with such enormous love, to the care of these two individuals. Their attitudes and actions will shape this little child's view, not only of them as parents, but more importantly, of God Himself. Their kindness, or lack of it, will shape the child's expectations of God. Their caring concern and attention, or lack of it, will speak a message that he or she is worthy of attention, value, and acceptance – or not.

Welcomed into the world?

The reality of the response to a child at their birth is another crucial element in the foundations of the child's internal thinking about their acceptability. Unfortunately, it is not always exactly as God would want it to be. I have already mentioned the issue of the gender of the baby. Any disappointment at the gender of the child is nowadays faced most often as a result of the twenty-week ultrasound scan. But for those of us of more senior years, our birth may have been the moment when the truth of our gender was at last known. For some it will have been a moment tinged with a profound sense of disappointment. We were not what had been hoped for. We were, just because of our gender, "a disappointment!" This attitude toward a child of whatever gestation, twenty weeks or full term, is deeply damaging to their sense of self-worth and well-being. If your gender, which is intrinsically part of you, is the very thing that makes you unacceptable, you can do nothing to change it. A sense of hopelessness can set in very early in the life of such a little one.

It is also unlikely, in these days of ultrasound scans, for a second baby in the womb to go unnoticed, but for those who were born before the 1970s this was sometimes the case. In those days twin pregnancies could go unnoticed until late in the pregnancy or even until the birth of the babies. During ministry, I have found that a second-born and unexpected baby seems especially prone to suffer from a deep feeling of being unrecognized, unacknowledged, unwelcomed, and therefore unaccepted.

Separation is not the best plan

The need for maternal bonding is so strong that taking a child from his mother soon after birth is potentially a rejecting experience for a baby. It can feel, to the child, as if he has been abandoned. Sometimes this separation is for the child's physical good, especially if there is a need for urgent medical attention. However, in the understandable focus on physical need, it is possible for the spiritual needs of the baby to be overlooked.

Time spent in a Special Care Baby Unit can save the life of a little one, especially if he is born very prematurely; however, at this critical stage he also desperately needs spiritual nurture to sustain him. He needs to be held close to his mother or father to bond with them, and to receive reassurance and a tangible sense of their love. He needs to be touched, spoken to, and delighted in. This means that early separation can lead to some deprivation of love and acceptance, just at a moment when the child is most in need of this reassurance. This may be especially so after the challenges of a difficult birth experience.

These days, in hospitals with baby units of this type, the staff recognize how essential this time of bonding is, and will encourage parents to visit their baby, talk to him, touch him (if this it at all possible), and even sing to him to establish as much contact as they can. They may not fully realize why this is so important, but they have seen by past experience the beneficial effects of these actions. For us this matter is clear. Since our human spirit is our life source and sustains our being, this feeding of the human spirit through bonding love and warm acceptance is vital and, together with any necessary medical help for the physical difficulties, gives the child the best opportunity to thrive.

> *The spirit of a man will sustain him in sickness,*
> *But who can bear a broken spirit?*
>
> (Proverbs 18:14)

Motive and manner

Surprisingly, the manner of birth also seems to be relevant. One day a lady who had been living with a low-level, chronic feeling of always being overlooked, and who reported that she felt an irrational sense of insecurity, came to me for prayer. Whilst seeking the roots of her problem, she mentioned she had been born by Caesarean section, and then the Holy Spirit revealed to her that she had been affected by a lack of acceptance at the time of her birth. She didn't really understand why this should be, since there was a medical reason why this type of delivery was necessary for her mother. However, it became clear that since the timing of her arrival was before she herself was prepared and ready to be born, she had perceived that she had been overlooked in the process. After prayer, she reported that she had lost the deep sense of insecurity, and felt as if her unheard heart cry had been answered.

Recently there has been a growing fashion among some mothers-to-be to choose to deliver their baby by what is called an "elective" Caesarean section. This is usually to facilitate the birth at a prearranged convenient time, suitable for both the hospital and the mother. If an essential emergency Caesarean section delivery may bring some possible negative effects for the baby, then choosing to go through this kind of birth with the motive of convenience must be of even greater concern. We have earlier discussed how the motive for doing something has a very significant effect on the spiritual outcome. It seems that babies who are "from [their] mother's womb untimely ripp'd," to quote Shakespeare's play *Macbeth*, may feel unconsidered, unacknowledged, and unprepared for life. Their inner deduction may be that they are a commodity to be organized, rather than a precious individual with their own special time to be born (Psalm 139:16; Ecclesiastes 3:2). God doesn't see them like that, and He certainly didn't plan for anyone to feel like that!

Adoption

In some cultures unwanted babies have been, and possibly still are, given up for adoption. If it is socially or culturally unacceptable for a single mother to keep her child, as it was for many decades in the UK, this may be her only option, regardless of her personal wishes to the contrary. Typically, such babies for adoption were taken from their mothers as soon as possible and put with foster parents. It was often the case that during whatever short time the mother had with her baby, for her own protection, she would try to maintain an emotional distance and to interact with him or her as little as possible. Indeed, she may have endeavored, in the months of her pregnancy, to reject the child and refrain from any acknowledgment of or bonding with the life growing within her womb. The hope was that this would, perhaps, make the parting with the child more bearable. However, the effect of such an attitude will have been devastating to the baby, as ministry with adults from such a background has often confirmed. The effect of being given away seems to have been even more poignant if the mother kept some of her children and rejected others. What greater wound to the human spirit can there be than to be rejected by your own birth mother, however sensible the decision she made seemed to be at the time?

I have met several adults, who were adopted as children, who struggle with a deep-seated and possibly unrecognized fear of rejection and abandonment. It has affected them throughout their lives and may drive them to strive to earn worth and significance. It may also cause them to use controlling behavior to ensure they are not abandoned again. The deep feelings even affect their Christian walk. It seems irrational and doesn't fit with their head knowledge about God, who says, "I will never leave you nor forsake you" (Hebrews 13:5), but the truth is that deep inside they fear that one day He just might.

Today it is more difficult to find a baby for adoption in the UK. But older children are being adopted from this country, and sometimes babies or children from overseas. Whatever nation these children are from, all adopted children have had a similar start in life: they have been orphaned or given away. In both cases they most probably will carry a deep wound of rejection. Even if the parents have died, the orphaned child often feels abandoned and rejected. In addition, many have been conceived outside of marriage and are suffering from the effects of the generational iniquity as we discussed in the last chapter.

It is a hard truth that being given up for adoption can cause the child damage, even though it may seem to be in the best interests of the child to go to a family who can give them better chances in life. Usually they are adopted by loving and caring parents who may have longed for a child for many years. Sadly, however, despite the continuing love and acceptance of their adoptive parents, such children often continue to harbor a sense of lack of acknowledgment and worth. They can struggle with ongoing deep feelings of rejection and all the associated problems and behaviors that this can bring. These feelings may go largely unexpressed or even unnoticed through childhood but can sometimes surface later, particularly in the teen years. I have prayed with more than one set of distraught parents who blamed themselves for having failed their adopted child when, in reality, the main root cause of their child's problems lay in the unrecognized damage of rejection from his or her earliest days of life.

Being different

A child born with a disfigurement will usually suffer from some measure of rejection. They may not be able to understand the words that people say about them, but they will "read" the spiritual atmosphere that greets them. The child themselves often seems to get lost behind the "problem" that they have. It may be a strawberry birthmark, noticed and commented on by visiting friends: "What a shame – she would be so pretty without that;" or a cleft palate that causes passers-by to stare, silently noting how ugly they find this baby to be; or a minor deformity that is hidden by parents because they feel embarrassed and ashamed of their less-than-perfect child. Of course, a child born with a more severe disability will almost certainly be affected by rejection, fuelling their deep feelings of being different and excluded from the acceptable "norm."

These little ones, who are considered imperfect by a world which is fixated on beauty and perfection, may fail to be accepted even in their own family. The rejections they have felt in their earliest days will eventually be reinforced during their childhood. They may have to endure rejecting looks from strangers in the street and rejecting comments from peers at school. But their Heavenly Father looks on them with the same unchanging love. He sees the beauty of His child: nothing can diminish His love. He loves and accepts each unique individual He has made, and each one belongs in His family just the same.

Experience builds my reality

We have seen that the circumstances and spiritual atmosphere of a child's birth and pre-birth time are important in forming foundational truths about his acceptability. To this we must add the effects of the early days of a child's life and his family circumstances, which are equally crucial. How the child is received, welcomed, and affirmed by the significant people in his life, especially by mother and father, grandparents and siblings, lays down an inner reality for each person. It is their personal "truth," a paradigm built up by the experiences of each day of their life. It seems unshakable, dependable, and unchangeable. In all honesty, even much later in life this inner truth may seem more true to them than the absolute truth of God's eternal Word.

It is a fact that the deepest feelings about being acceptable or unacceptable to God are usually rooted in these very early lessons learned from the experiences of life. Even as Christians, we find we have subconsciously assumed that the character of

God the Father is not far different from that which has been demonstrated by our own parents, especially our earthly father. This affects our ability to accept God for who He is and that He wants to give us His healing love. Put simply, past experiences limit our ability to know Him and receive what we need from Him.

We need to recognize what our own perception of God is really like. We need to understand not what we *think* we think but what deep inside we truly believe. This deep belief is based on what we, personally, received as we were growing up. Did my father still love me when I got it wrong? Was my father sympathetic when I showed my weakness, need, or fear? Did he give the impression he would fight for me and protect me as his valuable treasure? Was I only acceptable when I was good enough? These questions can help us expose the source of our erroneous and often subconscious beliefs about God that have been formed over our early years.

What shaped my worldview?

So what was your dad like? He may have been totally absent or preoccupied with his own activities. He may have been busy doing wonderful works as a doctor, pastor, or teacher. He may have worked long hours to make sufficient money for the family to survive. He may have been doing significant works for society, or even for the Lord. However, what a little child recognizes is that his dad is not there for *him* when he needs him. As adults we understand all the mitigating circumstances, but the child just feels the lack of practical and present fathering.

I wonder in how many homes the sound of the phone ringing signaled that Dad would be called away – the promise to play football or to read a bedtime story now forgotten or relegated to another time. Of course, there will be occasions when these things happen, even in the most caring of families, but consistently broken promises do not help us to grasp in our hearts the truth that God wants us to know – that He is faithful.

Or maybe it was Mum who was never there when the child got home from school and never had time to hear the problems of the day, or comfort the hurts from the playground scuffles. It seems to the child that his needs are not important, and that his worries are of little significance. He feels rejected because the things that concern him are ignored. How can anyone learn to trust and grow in the confidence that God is always there to unconditionally accept them and to help them in times of trouble, if their most significant relationships of life have shown otherwise?

It is not only the presence of parents, but also the quality of their presence that is critical. A child needs to be heard and allowed to speak without being shouted down. There needs to be time for physical tenderness, heart sharing, times of fun and laughter, and times of just being together. Harsh, unloving words are more obviously hurtful, but being in a family where there are never any words of love and encouragement spoken can be equally destructive. Total apathy towards a child brings the greatest wounding. It seems to say, "You aren't even worth acknowledging!" Sometimes even a bad relationship is better than no relationship at all, and perhaps this is why children from abusive homes would often rather stay at home than be separated from their parents. But the truth is that parents who regularly humiliate or abuse their children are planting the lie that they are valueless and can be used wrongly or discarded like rubbish.

Children need to be confident that as much as possible their needs, if not all their wants, will be considered and met. Sometimes they need to be given preference over activities or other people's demands on their parents' time. If this rarely or never happens, even in their own home, the child, unable to reason with adult rationale about the use of time, develops a feeling of rejection. This rejection results in deep beliefs along the lines of: "Everyone else is more important than me"... "My needs don't matter"... "I don't matter." These deep beliefs are lies of the enemy but can seem like a personal "truth." If they become reinforced and accepted as an indisputable truth, there is an opportunity for the enemy to hold a place of authority. This authority can be maintained by demonic presence, which is an unclean spirit. Jesus casts out demons to release people from such enemy authority in their lives. For example, He casts out a spirit causing infirmity in a woman in Luke 13:11. So a demon whose job function is to hold a person under the authority of the enemy's lies about their acceptability could be referred to as a "spirit of rejection." We will discuss this demonic aspect of the problem of rejection again later. No wonder the truth that God values each individual can seem to be unreal and totally unfathomable to such a child... and often still does, maybe years later in adulthood, even after he or she has become a Christian!

Happy Families!

To understand a little more about how family situations can instill wrong ideas about God into young lives, let's consider the happenings in three typical family homes in an ordinary street in your town.

At number 4 lives the Brown family. Dad works very hard and is a good provider for the family. But he works long hours and when he does get home he unwinds in front of the sports channel on the television all evening. He is not to be disturbed, Mum says. Secretly, she wants a quiet life, and his temper is easily roused when he is tired. The only time he shows interest is when the children do well at school. Then he averts his gaze from the TV for a few moments, says "Well done," and gives them a few precious seconds of undivided attention before returning to his sports program.

The picture of God unconsciously absorbed by the children each day is obvious. They receive the idea that God provides, but you should not ask anything extra from Him, or try to interrupt what He is doing. He is either busy or involved in His own interests (important spiritual stuff, of course), and He may be angry if you trouble Him at the wrong moment. Your only chance of acceptance, and much-needed attention, is to be clever enough to achieve in one of His spheres of interest. It probably seems that God only accepts high achievers and those who excel in spiritual things. Do you get the picture?

Next door, at number 6, lives the Smith family. Dad has left them. He went when little Sally was two months old. That was three years ago, and Daniel and Gavin, her elder brothers, have not seen him since. Mum says he was "a waster" anyway, and they are better off without him. The boys have always secretly wanted to see him again. They remember how he used to play football with them and they miss his rough-and-tumble games, but they dare not own their desires. Eventually they have had to push away their hopes that he will come back and, infected with Mum's constant poison of how rotten he was, they get on with being "the men of the household," as Granny calls them. Now they live independent lives and go their own way.

So what God-picture have they absorbed? God isn't there for you, and even if you really want Him to care for you He won't put in an appearance. Hope is bound to end in disappointment, so it is best not to hope. They are formulating attitudes for life: "I know what's best for me – who needs God?" This is definitely not the picture that God wanted to be painted by family life.

Three houses down the road, at number 12, is the Jones family. Dad is depressed because he has been out of work, off and on, over the last twenty years. When he does get a job he feels better for a few days, but then, with a little money in his pocket, he inevitably gets back to joining his drinking-buddies down at the pub. He is soon drinking away most of the money he has earned. Mum works hard to keep food on the table and goes to church each week. She says Dad would come if he wasn't unwell – never mentioning his drinking or his Sunday morning hangover! Dad eventually loses his job and returns to being on the dole. The atmosphere in the house is unpredictable. Dad's moods are erratic, depending where he is in the cycle of work, drinking, and depression. It feels unsafe to be around, so the children stay out with friends as much as possible. Mum is anxious about this and tries to use emotional blackmail to get them to stay at home more.

What picture of parenting are these children getting? It would not be unexpected if these children feel it is best to give God a very wide berth or to ignore Him altogether. Their God-picture is one full of fear and uncertainty, not security and care. Who knows what mood God will be in today? From Mum they also learn a lesson: When God says He loves you, He will probably try to manipulate and control you to get what He wants from you. These erroneous pictures will probably lead the children to decide it is best to do life without God, and to try to make their own places of security.

Of course, there may be a million variations on these themes of family life, but I am sure you can grasp the idea that I am trying to express.

The effect of sibling rivalry

A family is often more than Mum and Dad and one child. What about the child's relationship with siblings? God has no favorites; we are all special to Him. However, within a family there is, on occasion, a most favored child. Sometimes this is because of his or her gender, or because of some particular family likeness or trait. In the same family other children may be rejected for their particular idiosyncrasies, or even because they bear a striking resemblance to someone who is disliked in the family, e.g. a now despised ex-husband or former partner. A child who is rejected by parents will in turn probably reject one or more of his siblings.

A sibling of a favored child also feels "un-favored" by comparison and, hence, rejected in some way. Sibling rivalry that extends to bullying with words and actions, hatred, violence, and even murder is not unknown (Genesis 4:8). Joseph's brothers felt like this and we all know how they treated Joseph as a result of their feelings of being "un-favored" (Genesis 37:20). These continuing attitudes and actions make even the favored child feel rejected and unacceptable because of the effect of his or her favored status on the others in the family.

A foundational truth becomes rooted in children in such a family: God is like this. They may well believe Him to have favorites, or that on a whim He might reject someone because of some arbitrary part of their personality or looks.

The desire to be accepted is likely to drive children from backgrounds infected with rejection to try to earn acceptance. They may strive to get acceptance for what they achieve, instead of resting in an assurance of acceptance for who they are. This drive to win conditional acceptance will never satisfy the deep desire for true love, expressed through unconditional acceptance. We will discuss this issue further in a later chapter.

It is clear to me, from many hours of hearing people's personal stories, that many have had fathers, mothers, or significant carers that were not good God models. (Those of us who are parents may feel concerned that *we* have not been very good representatives of God's character for our children either. However, we can praise God that there is a pardon available for us, and healing for our children!) I am not pointing a finger at anyone for their inability to give us what we needed nor trying to apportion blame. Parents have, most often, failed in the God-modeling job because of their inability to give what they probably never received themselves: unconditional acceptance. We need to remember that our parents were suffering from wounds of rejection, and therefore had all the same associated problems that many of us are now trying to deal with.

Where do I belong?

We spoke earlier of children who have been taken into the care system because they have been orphaned, abandoned, or have been taken away from their parents. It is clear that a child left in the state care system and never placed in a loving home during all of their childhood will also suffer a deep sense of rejection. Despite perhaps the best intentions and efforts of professional carers, their feelings of being unaccepted and unacceptable can easily continue to be strengthened.

These feelings may be gradually embraced in order to find a sense of identity. The child may reason in his heart: "I am an outsider" and "I don't belong." In this way, life experiences of children may lead them to try to find a sense of belonging by joining a group of other similar "misfits." In this group they can find a kind of "family" substitute; a place of belonging of a sort. In the UK this is unlikely to be joining the Mafia (which is widely called "The Family" because it provides such a community), but it may easily be a rebellious gang, an antisocial group, a cult, a commune, or a brotherhood of drug-takers.

What a far cry from the true belonging that Father God wants them to find in His loving family, the belonging that will feed their human spirit and bring them security in the unfailing love and unconditional acceptance they so long for. Only God can heal these deep wounds. With God nothing is impossible (Luke 18:27).

Reality of past experiences and hope for the future

We need to be real about our own past. We need to consider how, and in what way, we were affected by a lack of acceptance or by outright rejection. We can then recognize who we need to forgive: those who have let us down and failed to provide the unconditional acceptance we needed to nurture us into our full personhood. In this way we bring the wounding of the past into the Kingdom of Light where there is healing. Then we can move on into receiving God's love and security in the deep places where a spirit of rejection has been ruling and reigning. There is a fresh, new start available to each of us if we are willing to walk the path of God's healing. We can put the past rejection and the associated lies behind us, not dismissed and buried, but forgiven, healed, and overwritten with God's truth. In Chapter 11 we will consider more fully how to pray into these issues.

The great thing is that God our Father is always available to re-parent us. He wants us to learn to respond to rejection in new ways. As we look at all these past difficulties we need to keep our heart set on the way forward. There is always hope in Jesus. He is the Healer and Teacher. We are looking back, but only to bring truth and light into the past so our present can be illuminated and we can step forward into a more glorious future.

Today's problem may have more than one cause

The fact is that as we are growing up there are often many levels of rejection attacking us, personally.

As an example, let's consider a little girl who is brought up with adoptive parents. In her life there are several differing threads of rejection to investigate. She will have been affected by any generational inheritance of rejection flowing down the family lines of her natural parents, and she will have been affected by their rejection of her when they gave her up for adoption. But she will also be affected by the way her adoptive parents have treated her, which may not always have been with true unconditional acceptance. In addition, she will have learned a lifestyle and expectation from her adoptive parents as they demonstrated dealing with their own rejection issues. Lastly, she will have been affected by numerous events of life that may have caused her to feel rejected. A picture of many parts, but none of them true to the truth of God's unconditional acceptance and faithful Father-heart for her.

Life experiences train the heart and mind

We are born the most receptive and un-patterned of all living beings.[1] We must, to a large extent, be programmed by those around us and by our experiences. Through this moment-by-moment learning program, we construct our framework of inner beliefs which give us our paradigm. Our sense of being unconditionally acceptable to others depends on the depositing of this truth in our lives, day by day, from our beginning. It seems as if God took a great gamble! He wholeheartedly desires that each of us should know the truth of His unconditional love, but He risks it all on the ability of others to demonstrate that truth to us. Before the Fall, God's plan was a foregone conclusion. Everything would have happened just as He intended and we would have learned clearly of His wonderful love. But we now live post-Fall, and the picture we have received of God's love has been twisted and distorted, as we have all learned to our detriment.

Many people – perhaps you are one of them – seem to find the truth that God loves them without condition almost impossible to grasp. They may know this to be correct from Bible verses, although some even seem to doubt this. They may be able to quote the relevant verses, but they cannot hold onto the truth as applying to them personally. They feel unable to believe that He could really truly be that sort of God. Maybe the realization that our picture of God has been laid down by the experiences of our family life will help us to recognize that our problem is that we are disabled by our inner thinking. The good news is that although we will need a very special type of healing for these inner beliefs about God, He is more than willing and able to accomplish this work in us, so we *can* live in the wonderful security of His amazing love.

But before we begin to look at how we can receive this amazing, life-transforming healing, there are one or two more contributing factors to the problem of rejection that we need to understand. Outside family life there is a big, wide, and trouble-filled world where there are other relationships and circumstances which may also afflict us with a sting of rejection. The next chapter will consider some of these other aspects of life which have, perhaps, reinforced our sense of being unacceptable.

Notes

1. Sue Gerhardt, *Why Love Matters: How Affection Shapes a Baby's Brain* (Routledge, 2004, reprinted 2008).

CHAPTER 5

The Reality of Life – Will Everyone Reject Me?

Relationships can heal or hurt

Relationships are very important to us. It is through our relationships that we receive acknowledgment and affirmation of our worth and a sense of belonging. We have been made for relationship: we are made in God's image (Genesis 1:26). He is relational, in His tripartite being: He is Father, Son, and Holy Spirit.

As a child matures, their circle of acquaintances widens. There are more people who could potentially show them love and acceptance but, alas, also more people with the power to hurt and reject them. Loving and being loved is what we need and desire, but love also makes us vulnerable to being hurt. This hurt may come because people are inconsistent or fickle in their love toward us, or because someone we love chooses to reject us.

One of the unexpected situations that can cause a wound of rejection is the death of someone significant to us. The death of a friend or loved one is a significant event in anyone's life, but this is especially so if the person has been the main focus of our love, or if they have been present for much, or all, of our life. Their commitment to us, and cherishing of us, will have undoubtedly brought us a sense of worth and value. We have seen that children depend greatly on their significant relationships for their sense of well-being and security. In these cherishing relationships they find a place of belonging. But what happens if a parent or sibling dies when a child is very young?

Having ministered and talked to adults about the reality of their feelings when they have been through bereavement, I have gained some valuable insights. Rationally, adults understand that the person they have lost did not choose to die, but what is surprising is that many who are bereaved report that they feel an irrational sense of abandonment, as if they have been personally rejected. This can also result in an unexpected feeling of anger at being deserted. If rational adults feel these uninvited feelings, then surely children in the same situation are likely to feel the same.

Childhood grief

It is therefore logical to assume that children, even very young children, will feel the loss of someone significant as a very personal abandonment. Many people who have lost a parent in early childhood suffer from this deep sense of rejection, which can continue unrecognized into their adult life. They may have the knowledge of the past event but, because they are rationalizing that bereavement is clearly not an intentional abandonment, they are unaware of the wound of rejection suffered at that time. This unrecognized inner hurt may have been affecting their life ever since. There will be a similar effect from loss through the death of a sibling, friend, or grandparent, or any other significant person in the child's life.

The rejection might be made more painful if, in their own grief, the remaining adults do not feel able to talk about the loss, therefore leaving the child to try to make sense of it all alone.

A lady once told me how her mother had taken down all the photos of her little sister, after she had died in hospital from meningitis. No one ever explained to her what had happened to her sister, or mentioned the little girl in conversation. They never even spoke her name again. They lived in a rural area and the two sisters had been constant companions, playing together every day. She was now left alone and isolated. Her mother took to her bed, lost in her own grief, so that the child's sense of abandonment was never in any way eased or comforted. She felt rejected by her sister leaving her, and rejected by her mother's silence and the withdrawal of her presence. She reasoned that the only explanation for all that had happened was that she was too bad to be loved. So she tried harder to be good, never mentioning her sister, to keep in her mother's "good books," and squashed down her feelings of grief. She hoped that by being good enough she might win back her mother's love. In adult life, this lady became a perfectionist who always felt she was the guilty one and to blame when other people were sad, whatever the true reason for their feelings. She was an insecure person who only found her sense of belonging in being in control of everyone and everything around her. She had never realized that part of the cause of her control problem lay in the death of her little sister.

The greatest loss for a child is that of a relationship in which they have felt unconditionally accepted – often this has been with a loving grandparent. One lady talked to me about the death of her granny when she was nine years old.

She had always been the one who listened to me; she had time for me and she thought I was special. She used to say, "You are my treasure!" When she died I felt totally abandoned. It felt as if she had gone away and left me all alone. Alone in a world that didn't care about me, about what I thought or wanted, with no one who thought I was a treasure.

The pain of the rejection she felt was not anyone's fault. It was not caused by sin, but by the circumstances of life in a fallen world, where death and separation is endemic.

Separation and abandonment

There are other kinds of loss that can lead to feelings of rejection that we need to consider. A young woman whose family had moved sixteen times during her school years told me how she always felt that her fellow pupils were pleased when her family moved away and she left the school. She felt as if they had rejected her although, in fact, she had been the one to leave each time. Even though she had made friends at most of the different schools she had attended, she never really expected to be accepted, or felt secure in any friendship. Her feelings about her past life today were somewhat different from the reality. She felt that during her childhood everyone had rejected her. Although she understood rationally that this was not so, she couldn't explain the inner certainty that they had all abandoned her. As we talked more about her life, it became apparent that she had been close to an elderly great-aunt who had looked after her a great deal in her babyhood, but died when she was four years old. This was the real root of her oversensitivity to being abandoned; and all the later loss of friends, when she had left each school, was feeding this deep sense of rejection. No one had intended her to feel this way, but the repeated loss of loved ones had been perceived by the child as others choosing to reject her.

Some children are sent away to boarding school by parents who are keen for the best intellectual education possible for their child. It is easy to understand why this may seem a good idea. Perhaps the family is living abroad and there is limited educational possibility, or the family tradition is for the children, possibly just the sons, to go to a specific noteworthy private school. I have prayed with many people who have gone to boarding school, and even those who have attended good and caring schools often seem to have been damaged by a sense of rejection caused by being "sent away." I once prayed with a lady whose parents were missionaries in an African country. She had been sent home, aged three, to start at boarding school so that her parents could be free to get on with their Kingdom work. My heart grieved for this lady, but she didn't initially feel they had done anything wrong. I couldn't help but feel that, perhaps, her parents had missed one of the major tasks that God had asked them to do. Their work in Africa was no doubt important, but their modeling of God's unconditional acceptance and value for their daughter had been relegated to a very poor second on their list of priorities. This lady came because she had a problem which was hampering her Christian walk. She wondered why she always felt so worthless and suffered with such low self-esteem that she was unable to do the things that she felt God had called her to do. When we asked God to show her how she really felt as a little child being sent away, the floodgates opened and she sobbed out her deep hurt of rejection. Healing came as I put my arm around her to console her, and spoke the words of her Heavenly Father's comfort into her human spirit.

Where do I fit in?

The fear of not belonging becomes increasingly important as children become more aware of being "different" from the crowd. This may mean pleading with Mum for the right type of trainers, so they are "in" and not "out." It may mean having to have a particular sort of jeans or a designer-label jacket, having the most up-to-date iPod, or knowing the latest jokes. The fear of rejection is a very strong motivator.

Children with disabilities or obvious physical characteristics are often mercilessly ridiculed and called names: "Carrots," "Four-eyes," "Fatty," "Beanpole" all come to mind as examples from my school days. (Sadly, I was not only called names by others, but sometimes I was a name-caller too!) These names devalue the person on the receiving end, reducing them to one particular and ridiculed aspect of their personhood. Many adults today are able to remember being called names like these, and may still cringe inside at the memory. Some have dealt with the pain of these old rejections, but others have buried their hurt, ashamed by the power it still seems to exert. But buried hurts stay alive and fester, causing us to continue to be shaped and motivated by the unrecognized pain and associated inner beliefs about our unacceptability.

We need to ask Jesus to help us face these old wounds of rejection. His desire is to set us free and to bring comfort and healing to those deep hurts which date back to our schooldays and beyond. We are still bearing the scars in our inner being and it is never too late to receive the restoration we need. He is waiting to bring deep healing for us if we will ask Him for the courage to face the pain.

The challenge of teenage years

As we continue to look at the possible underlying roots of the rejection that affects our thinking today, it is important not to overlook the often challenging teenage years. Most young people face some insecurity associated with leaving childhood and becoming an adult. It is often a time of self-consciousness as the body changes physically, and this self-consciousness may be exacerbated if there is teasing from siblings or parents which draws attention to these changes, or conversely to the lack of development.

At this time, young people need all the reassurance possible as they begin to assess their acceptability, not just as a person, but as a sexually mature human being. The desire to be found attractive, especially to the opposite sex, becomes a focus of attention. Fears of being found unacceptable add pressure to buried self-rejection and feelings of worthlessness. Desperate to overcome the self-doubt which is the fruit of past rejections, a young person may embrace strange attitudes and behaviors to try to achieve acceptance and affirmation from their peers. These behaviors are often those which their parents find unacceptable. This may result in further rejection from their parents, especially if the behavior seems to them to be antisocial or rebellious. Such a response merely compounds the teenager's rejection problem, and fuels the downward spiral that is rooted in a deep doubt about their personal acceptability.

This fallen world, under the sway of Satan, the ruler of this world, as Jesus describes him, is filled with people who are suffering with the ongoing wounds of rejection (John 14:30). The hurt of rejection is especially strong when we are betrayed or abandoned by someone we considered to be a close or special friend. Teenagers, in particular, can experience an acute sense of abandonment when they are "dumped" by a boyfriend or girlfriend. "Jilting" may be an old-fashioned term, but the pain of abandonment is still the same today. Miss Haversham, in Dickens's *Great Expectations*, jilted on her wedding day, sat in her fading wedding dress all the rest of her life, trapped in her rejection. She couldn't or wouldn't move forward into life. Her rejection had become her identity and remained so for all of her years of life. This may seem extreme, but many people are still wearing the unseen clothes of past rejections in a similar way.

Broken marriages affect everyone

In our society many young people live in broken families or with step families. We have become used to such arrangements, and they may seem to result in reasonably happy and satisfactory living arrangements. However, broken families were not part of God's original plan, so behind such a present-day situation lies the pain of a past separation and the associated issues of rejection that, sadly, does not affect only the adults who were involved. Children and young adults, alike, often suffer as badly from the effects of their parents' broken relationship as from their own relationship breakdowns.

Let us consider the effect of marriage breakdown on all those involved.

Occasionally the two people involved may have just drifted apart, and can perhaps rationalize why the breakdown of their relationship has happened. They may have made a mutual decision to part, but there can still be a sense of failure and feelings of having been "not good enough" to meet their partner's needs. Although this is less likely to be the cause for the breakdown of a Christian marriage, there are those who have suffered in this way before becoming believers. They may experience an added problem: the rejecting disapproval of legalistic religious people who seem to imply that divorce is an unforgivable sin.

In any case, the breakdown of a long-term relationship, particularly a covenant relationship of marriage, brings a devastating sense of rejection to at least one of the people involved. Sometimes both people feel equally rejected by their partner. It is very painful to come to the realization that someone who once loved and cared for you now wants to be apart from you, despite the heartache it causes you. Their desire to be with someone else or to return to their single life leads to the grief of abandonment.

However, if there has been a sudden revelation of an extramarital affair, or a totally unexpected decision by one person to end the relationship, then the other will feel devastatingly rejected. "After twenty-six years of marriage," a man said to me one day, "she just told me she was leaving to live abroad. Without any explanation she packed her bags and left on that very day." He was left dazed, bewildered, angry, and feeling totally abandoned. He assumed his wife would see sense and come back, but after a few weeks he began to realize she might not. His confidence evaporated and he began to drink to drown his sorrows. He felt utterly rejected as he faced the truth that she had made the decision to go forward to fulfill her dream, and he just didn't fit into that dream – he needed to be ditched! Rationalizing these actions as her selfishness helped his head to understand, but his inner feelings were unaffected by the mental gymnastics! Whether it is a slow decline of commitment and love, or a sudden revelation of a betrayal, the pain of the rejection is the same. Broken trust causes a deep wound of rejection.

Many young people these days have parents who no longer live together. The separation of a child from a parent they love is very painful, especially if they are unable to maintain significant regular contact. If there is also an aggressive and bitter attitude between parents, this is likely to cause the child extra pain, and further fuel their sense of isolation and rejection. It is possible that children affected by divorce can be reassured that both parents love and accept them, and that they have not personally been rejected. But this is a challenge for parents who are themselves hurting and rejected. The negative effects on children can be minimized by explaining what has happened, in a way they can understand, and reassuring them that the breakdown is not in any way their fault.

Children may need help with their feelings of anger about the circumstances. Anger is a very common response to feelings of rejection, and this is partly righteous anger, because God is also angry about the situation. The pain of the injustice of rejection and betrayal is not what He planned for anyone.

He intended us to enjoy the benefits of feeling secure in the unconditional acceptance and harmony of those whom we love. Understanding that God knows how they feel and is not shocked at their feelings can help children to realize that it is all right to feel angry. Unfortunately, at a time of extreme emotional turmoil it is often very hard for parents to help their children to deal with their emotions, because they are struggling with their own overwhelming feelings.

Redundancy and workplace rejection

For many people, part of their sense of worth and acceptance is gained from their position and value in their place of employment. There were days when a man joined a firm as a lad and had job security for as long as he wanted, providing he did what was required of him. However, in today's world many people have had to suffer from the rejection of having been made redundant. During the recent "credit crunch," redundancies have been like missiles hitting unsuspecting workers in areas previously assumed to be secure places of employment. There are some unfortunate people who have been made redundant on more than one occasion: rejection building upon rejection. Redundancy, especially when it is due to reorganization or business circumstances, is not usually intended as a personal rejection. However, more often than not, it feels and hurts like a personal rejection. It can lead to a deep sense of worthlessness and despair. In addition, after losing their job, many have gone on to apply for countless new positions only to be rejected every time, and often without even the courtesy of a written refusal letter. Rejected and feeling worthless, it is easy for what little confidence they had to evaporate, and so the cycle of unemployment continues for many.

This rejection from the working world is especially painful for those who have found significance and acceptance in their workplace, or who have based their self-worth on success in their chosen employment or profession. Often suffering from childhood rejections and with consequential feelings of unacceptability, they drive themselves to gain significance in their job. Striving for acceptance becomes their life's motive. Such people have sought a sense of value and security through the affirmation and acclaim of their employer and peer group. However, the conditional acceptance they have worked for will never meet their deep innermost need. In a world that offers only conditional acceptance, we are forced to try to gain security by what we do rather than who we are.

In the next chapter we will look at how many of life's experiences, from our earliest days, develop our tendency to settle for *conditional acceptance* as a way to feel better about ourselves. We need to consider further how damaging this counterfeit type of acceptance is... it is definitely not the "real thing!"

CHAPTER 6

Deceptive Lessons from the School of Life – Are You Good Enough to be Accepted?

How can I get acceptance?

We all do it; it just comes naturally. We strive to gain acceptance, and to avoid rejection. Why? We do it because we don't like pain, and rejection hurts. We do it in a multitude of ways. We work at getting letters after our name, at being the best athlete, the low-handicap golfer, a *cordon bleu* chef, the most committed pray-er, the super-diligent carer, or simply the best at whatever might help us to feel we're climbing up the rungs of the acceptance ladder. Without realizing what we are doing, we are trying to push away our doubts about our acceptability and to persuade ourselves that we can be good enough to be accepted. Striving for conditional acceptance is a treadmill that exhausts those that enter into it. Like a hamster, we go round and round and go nowhere. The inner problem is never solved because we have not realized what the problem really is!

Conditional acceptance is the way of the world. And if we lack a foundation of true unconditional acceptance, it is so easy to fall under its appeal. We confuse our true need of unconditional acceptance for "who we are" with the seeming benefits of earning conditional acceptance for "what we do." We strive to earn the right to belong and to gain the illusive feeling of security. The hidden agenda for many of us is: "If I can just do well enough and meet the standards to be good enough, then I will be OK." What a far cry this is from the truth that God wants us to understand: the truth that we are loved for who we are, each of us a unique and special individual.

We all know that a little one needs physical nourishment to grow strong in body, but we have seen how he also needs the love and unconditional acceptance of his parents for his spiritual well-being and so he will grow strong in spirit. His human spirit is tuned to receive life-giving spiritual nurture from the earliest days of his life. Even when he is too young to understand the words spoken or to focus on the expressions on faces around him, he is spiritually aware of his parents' feelings toward him. Being unconditionally accepted makes him feel safe, connected, and recognized for the person he is. But a painful, fear-filled, lost feeling of insecurity comes when he is rejected. As he grows and develops, he is subconsciously recording, deep in his innermost being, his acceptability rating. Is he up to the mark? Is he safe? Is his life under threat? He is hungry for acceptance and security but feels pain and fear when he is rejected.

Fear is a great motivator

Since lack of acceptance causes a child to feel insecure and vulnerable, he fears rejection and the pain it brings. He will develop feelings of fear if he perceives that either Mummy or Daddy is withdrawing their love from him. Some very sensitive babies and toddlers will cry when a parent raises their voice in disapproval. Of course it is necessary for parents to discipline their children, but we are talking about something more than appropriate chastising for wrongdoing. If one of his parents should be very angry, shouting or even aggressive toward him, the child will recognize this as an expression of their displeasure and feel it as rejection. He may be distressed if he seems to have been abandoned (even if this is not so in actuality). Prolonged separation from his primary love source is a major hurt for a little one to bear. He will do everything he can to avoid this pain and the vulnerable, unsafe feeling it brings.

It doesn't take long before a small child begins to formulate a way to minimize this pain. It is not in any way conscious, but comes from the subconscious inner being. He perceives that when the people around him are pleased with what he does, they seem to become more loving toward him. He also perceives that the reverse is true. In their loving attention lies his hope of security and a minimizing of the pain of possible future disapproval. Of course, not all parents send this message to their children but, sadly, many do. The child learns from the world a damaging lesson: being good will bring you acceptance. The cruel truth is that it is only acceptance of a kind. It is not the unconditional acceptance that he really needs, and which would give him the true security of knowing that he is loved for himself, whatever he does. No, this is a highly deceptive but seemingly close relative: it is *conditional acceptance*. Conditional acceptance will demand his servitude. Increasingly, he will work to stay in the "good books" of those around him. It is a recipe for a life striving to be good enough, and will usually lead to the slavery of people-pleasing. His behavior may look good, but there is a deep unseen problem. Inside he has increasing doubts about his worth and acceptability just for who he is: the person God made him to be.

Fear leads to control

In this way, a child becomes open to control: the control of conditional acceptance. This kind of acceptance, in reality, rejects him for who he is and accepts only how he behaves.

Conditional acceptance is a kind of hidden rejection that proves to be poisonous to the person's innermost being.

Of course, Mum and Dad may be as unaware of this hidden problem as the child himself. They may be congratulating themselves on the obedience of their child and his desire to please them. But in fact they may unknowingly be laying down the foundations of a belief in the child that to receive acceptance you need to strive to get it by good works. This child will increasingly be unable to trust that he is loved and acceptable when he fails at any task. He will certainly not expect to be loved when he is naughty, and this expectation will probably be reinforced over time by his parents. He is learning that love and acceptance are conditional on reaching a standard. The battle with the sense of conditional acceptance which many believers still face in adulthood today, has often begun when they were very young.

Discipline is an essential part of a child's parenting. The writer to the Hebrews tells us this fact clearly and urges parents to correct their children when necessary.

"For whom the LORD loves He chastens" ...
But if you are without chastening ... then you are illegitimate and not sons.

(Hebrews 12:6, 8)

I am in no way suggesting that a child should be left unaware when he has behaved badly: he needs to know clearly what is right and what is wrong. The behavior is unacceptable, but the child is more than just his present bad behavior. Even in the moment of appropriate discipline he needs to be reassured that he is not being rejected. *He* is not bad, but his *behavior* is bad. This is challenging for parents, but with God's help this distinction can be made: the distinction between the sin and the sinner. The sin is wrong, but the sinner is still unconditionally accepted for the God-created person he is. Jesus demonstrates how this can be achieved as He relates to the woman dragged to meet Him when she had been caught in the act of adultery (John 8:1–12). Everything that Jesus does and says is motivated out of His love and unconditional acceptance of her. He looks down at the ground, averting His eyes, whilst everyone else stares in disapproval. His comment makes it clear that she is a sinner like everyone else: no one is able to cast the first stone. He values her and treats her with dignity, but clearly confronts her sin and tells her to "go and sin no more" (John 8:11).

The slave mentality

God grieves for His children, of all ages, caught in this never-ending struggle to try to earn acceptance. He made each of us for His unconditional acceptance, but so often these early life experiences continue to undermine our belief that this could really be true. Inside each of us a heart cry echoes, "Is it possible that I could be loved and accepted just for being who I am?" Our Heavenly Father's intention is that we would delight to do what is right and to do our best at any task, out of the confident place that whatever the result, we are still totally accepted and secure in His love. However, Satan delights to encourage conditional acceptance. It forces us to try to prove our worth and to strive for what is, in fact, freely ours: the immense and unchangeable love of our Father God. The roots of this striving are in the carnality of fallen man, who is trying through his own wisdom to make himself acceptable by his own efforts. By buying into a life of conditional acceptance, we increasingly turn away from God's better way and come under the rule of Satan, the father of lies.

You are the children of your father, the Devil, and you want to follow your father's desires. From the very beginning he was a murderer and has never been on the side of truth, because there is no truth in him. When he tells a lie, he is only doing what is natural to him, because he is a liar and the father of all lies.

(John 8:44 GNB)

Unrecognized, conditional acceptance has become normative in this fallen world. Emotional pressure, through the threat of withdrawal of love and approval, is often used to get children, and vulnerable adults, to do what others require of them. This may be especially so during the formative years of a child's life. However, the threat of more rejection does little to help the child to feel secure and does a great deal to make them more anxious.

This cycle of striving to please and being afraid of rejection may start with "potty" training. The child who continually fails in this endeavor, or who wets the bed at night, might be bombarded with humiliating words and actions, which increases his sense of rejection, anxiety, and distress. If an anxious child fears rejection he will become more anxious, and thus less able to do what is asked of him. It can be a vicious and self-defeating cycle. The acceptability the child craves rests on success, but this success seems to be beyond his present ability, for whatever reason.

This pattern may be repeated in many areas of a child's life and is especially common in school. Being weak and unable in one key subject can, in this way, feed the low self-worth of the student, who sees himself increasingly as a "worthless and useless" person. (I wonder what it was for you – mathematics, spelling, or art, maybe?) Inability to achieve a required standard becomes, in his perception, the same as rejecting him as a person. Trying harder leads to increased striving, stress, and anxiety.

The problem of trying to please others

The need to be accepted and the associated striving for conditional acceptance can affect many areas of our lives. For instance, when parents split up, many children think that they themselves are somehow to blame, and they feel very unsure and insecure. They will often strive, initially, to try to do what pleases both of their separated parents in the hope that this will win them acceptance and an increased sense of security. But in many cases they find it is impossible to win acceptance from both at the same time and this can be very stressful indeed, especially if pleasing one leads to displeasing the other. The result is that, however hard they try, they seem doomed to failure. At this difficult time, they are most in need of the security of unconditional acceptance from their parents, but if they have only ever had conditional acceptance they have little chance of being able to receive the real comfort and assurance they need on the inside. The only possibility open to them is to reject one parent and please the other, just to be able to alleviate the stress of trying to please two often opposing masters.

Even with their best efforts to win at least conditional acceptance, children often fail to find what they so desperately seek. They may continually suffer from a barrage of angry and rejecting words. Some will renew their efforts and strive harder, while others may give up trying to be accepted and turn instead to angry rebellion.

Some time ago I prayed with a young woman who, despite having tried very hard to please her dad and win his acceptance, felt she had failed him. She had done her best in her studies and had done what was necessary at home, but had been subjected to his violent attacks, during one of which he had broken her arm. She felt she hadn't done well enough, and was prepared to try harder to please him and win his love. Such was her desperation for acceptance that she couldn't see that he was at fault, but instead blamed herself. However, another young woman, whose father had similarly been critical and demanding of her school work, gave up her efforts, leaving home and school as soon as she was legally able, and dropped out of life to find acceptance, of a kind, in a drug-taking subculture.

Conditional acceptance breeds dysfunction

School life has the potential to further encourage a leaning towards working for conditional acceptance and a striving mentality. Praises and acclaim go to those who achieve success. Attention and prizes go to those who come top. Being the best, it is clear to all, is what is needed; but an inability to achieve, with all the humiliation that follows failure, is to be avoided. For the less able child the truth rings clear: "Success brings acceptance, and you are not in that category – you are a reject." That is the message that many receive in their school years.

Success with your peers

The deep longing for real acceptance frequently generates desperation to belong somewhere – anywhere! "If only I could find a group of people with whom I could find acceptance..." In school years this often becomes a compelling issue. Children increasingly strive to be accepted by and belong to a chosen group. It may be a specific team, a uniformed club, the "clever ones," the "sporty ones," or even the "naughty ones!" Being left out and alone is rejection and it hurts. How many boys longed to be picked for the school football team, or even to be included in the kick-about game in the local park? One man told me how he had felt many years ago in the playground at his school. The best footballers were always the captains, and all the boys who wanted to play lined up against a wall to be chosen in turn by the captains. "I was rather fat," he said, "and not very good at football, but I desperately wanted to be included. I used to be silently pleading with God, 'Please don't let me be the last one chosen.'" As he spoke, the tears began to well up in his eyes. He owned that he *was* invariably the last one left; and the captain who was unfortunate enough to have to "choose" him, as the last available option, always made his feelings very obvious.

Eventually, of course, the pain became too bad and he turned his back on sports, especially football, and admitted he had always hated it since. It happened so long ago, but the pain of the rejection had never been released and was still very much alive.

Humiliation and ridicule

It isn't just other children who have the power to hurt with words. Many have suffered at the hands of teachers, who have sought to exert authority over a class by humiliating individual children, especially those who don't reach the required standard. No doubt the motive of such a teacher will have been to inspire the child to do better, but he or she was unknowingly making it more difficult for the pupil to succeed. In the past, teachers' attempts to get good results by any means often led them to use verbal abuse, or worse.

Caning is not allowed in the UK these days, but many in previous generations were humiliated by public punishment sessions. I remember having the wooden-backed blackboard eraser thrown at me in anger for getting a spelling wrong in class. Luckily it missed me, but others were less fortunate. I remember fellow pupils who were made to stand for a whole lesson on their chair because they were unable to recite the necessary times-table. I can still see their ever-reddening faces and squirming gestures, as they tried to escape the staring gaze of the furious teacher and the gloats of all the rest of the class. Maybe these things don't happen in today's schools; I certainly hope not, because such experiences teach us that failure brings rejection, not just of my poor work, but of "me." It may be necessary, of course, to encourage and instruct the child to improve their work, but there should be at the same time a valuing of the child. This kind of humiliating rejection is a sort of abuse: it says, "You are no good." It declares, "You are of no value and your needs don't matter: you are beyond hope and help. You are, simply, not worth the bother!" No wonder we strive to be good enough and sometimes drive ourselves to exhaustion trying to prove our worth.

Violence, humiliation, and words of derision bring rejection and stab deeply into the human spirit of a child. Even words like "You're stupid," "You'll never be any good," or "You're letting the whole class down" have the potential to pierce the hearts of young people and cause a wound that can fester for years. If there is already damage from an earlier lack of unconditional acceptance, these pronouncements, and others like them, will reiterate what the child already fears – that they are simply not good enough, full stop. They are unacceptable and should be utterly rejected. The inner belief of being "a reject" grows in the fertile ground of conditional acceptance, bearing bad fruits in both attitudes and behavior for years to come. Somehow the standards are never quite achievable, so the label "Reject" becomes more and more securely fastened to us.

Trying to avoid the pain

Our striving and self-effort to win acceptance, and our attempts to find a sense of belonging, have a very significant effect on our daily lives. Next we need to consider how these deep feelings of unacceptability and rejection have motivated our behavior in the past, and still do now. This will require us to look with honesty and with God's help at the daily record of our lives. He lovingly watches over us each day and knows how we behave and why. The truth is that often our actions, to try to alleviate the pain of rejection or to protect ourselves from future rejection, are not in accordance with the way God would want us to behave. As Elihu puts it to Job:

> *Take heed, do not turn to iniquity,*
> *For you have chosen this rather than affliction.*   (Job 36:21)

Instead of helping our plight, our iniquitous behaviors give us another problem. These ungodly actions, which we so readily turn to, are what we will consider in the next chapter.

My Response to Rejection – What Else Could I Do?

Rejection lays down distorted inner beliefs

We have been exploring the painful truth that many of us have suffered in the past from wounds of rejection. Jesus said, "In the world you will have tribulation" (John 16:33), and we have surely all found that He never said a truer word! (In reality He never said a less true word either, since all He said was absolute truth!) It is clear that rejection hurts us; it steals our joy in childhood and limits our potential to relate to others. We have seen, too, that we can get into the lifestyle of striving for conditional acceptance. However, there are other serious hidden consequences of past rejection that continue to have a detrimental effect on our well-being today. Early incidents of rejection in our lives not only hurt our feelings and starve us of the necessary nurture of acceptance, but also cause us to form an internal understanding of why the rejection happened to us. We begin to build a structure of inner thoughts and beliefs that will underpin our future lives.

In one of the parables that Jesus told, He said we should build our house on a rock (Matthew 7:24–27). The implication is that our lives are the house, and His Truth is the Rock. We need His Truth as our life foundations. Building on sand (anything other than His Truth), He warns, will result in an unstable house and there could be a catastrophic collapse when difficult times come. Now, when sand is pressed down it can produce a soft type of sandstone which seems to be firm – a bit like rock – but is, in reality, easily eroded by wind or water. It may feel as if it is rock to the ordinary person, but it certainly isn't a good, solid, and true foundation. Do you see the analogy? What "truths" (perhaps we could call them "inner beliefs") is the house of your life built on? Are they the "inner beliefs" that agree with The Truth (The Rock), or are they your own brand of "truth" that may well be nothing more than pressed-down sand – in short, unstable untruths and lies? The reality is that many people have built their life-house on what feels like a sort of truth but is at best half-truths and sometimes nothing more than lies.

These inner beliefs are the foundation of our lives. If our foundation is lies and not God's truth, we cannot build a solid, righteous, and strong life. God's truth says we are unconditionally acceptable and always will be, but the inner beliefs we have (which are lies we have formulated from our experiences) often tell us something quite different. We have seen how these inner lies can cause us to strive to prove our acceptability, which may lead to driven-ness. But equally well, these inner beliefs can cause us to live with the hopelessness of low self-esteem and worthlessness all our days. These hidden lies are the roots that now feed the ongoing problem of feeling rejected and isolated. Jesus says that truth is essential for freedom and so exposing these lies will be very important.

> *... you shall know the truth, and the truth shall make you free.*
>
> (John 8:32)

> *... You desire truth in the inward parts ...*
>
> (Psalm 51:6)

My "truth" motivates my behavior

So, how do we recognize these erroneous inner beliefs? These thoughts seem so natural and so very "true," because they have been laid down through chronic or acute experiences of life. What is more, over the years, we have developed complex ways of thinking, out of these inner beliefs, and these patterns of thought have developed our behaviors and reactions. It is in working backwards from our behavior that these inner lies can be exposed and recognized. If we understand how this framework of our lives has been constructed over the years, then today we can ask God to begin to unearth these untruths that are supporting and sustaining our feelings of being rejected.

Let us examine first how beliefs and behaviors are interrelated. Take, for example, the issue of how we deal with our emotions. Small children start out in life being very real about their emotions. They initially find it hard to hide their feelings, but this can be changed if they face rejection when they are real about them. For instance, imagine a little boy who is honest about his fear of the dark and starts to cry. If he is consistently rejected by his dad for crying, because it is "sissy to cry," then this may well have consequences in his behavior for the rest of his life. The pain of the rejection makes him want to avoid the emotions that brought the rejection. He will begin to reason that it is safer to deny his emotions or, better still, to avoid any emotional situations. His unconscious thinking is that emotions are harmful to him, because they provoked the pain of the rejection. This may lead him to attitudes and behaviors such as denying that he has any feelings, or withdrawing from relationships to avoid any chance of emotional hurt.

Later in life this boy could easily become a man who finds that he is unable to form a deep or intimate relationship, because such a relationship demands emotional involvement. His behaviors have been distorted by his inner beliefs, which in turn were laid down by his past experiences.

If the same boy has been afraid of Dad's anger and disapproval and has engaged in desperate attempts to win Dad's affirmation, then as an adult he may be careful to avoid any sort of disagreement, because this may draw possible rejection. He will have adopted a people-pleasing attitude to avoid the negative emotional responses of others which could lead to rejection. Confrontation will be avoided at all costs by this man and he may believe himself to be a peacemaker, whilst, in truth, he is motivated by fear of rejection.

One lady came for prayer because she had suddenly recognized that she was terrified to be living alone. I asked her if she had any idea where this fear came from. She said she had never had the fear before, but during the conversation she mentioned that as a little girl she had suffered from some physical abuse from a neighboring child, when she had been left alone to play in the garden, her parents having gone out briefly. It became clear that she had formulated an inner belief: "I am not safe alone – I will be abused," and this had settled into her heart. This had become a foundation for her life and had affected her behavior. She was usually very active. She helped others, had a ministry of hospitality with missionaries on furlough, ran coffee mornings, had student lodgers, and generally did wonderful work for the Church. She had always thought that she was just a busy sort of person. However, she had been unwell and so had stopped doing all these things for a season. It was during this time that God showed her a reality that had been hidden to her. She was, in part, doing all these things out of a foundation of fear: fear of being alone. Her inner beliefs that she was unsafe alone were exposed, and God could minister His truth to her in a new way to cancel out the inner lie. The words, "He is my refuge and my fortress … in Him I will trust" (Psalm 91:2) sank deep into her heart and she never suffered with the fear again.

Much of our behavior is motivated by our past wounds of rejection, and fear of feeling the pain of rejection again. Our inner beliefs and their associated thinking patterns form the

basis and motivator of how we behave. They also form the
foundational truths about how we feel about ourselves and how
we relate to others around us each day.

Exposing the lies and preparing for change

There is wisdom in recognizing what we cannot change and
accepting it. But I believe that God wants us to recognize and
take responsibility for what we *can* change. The fact that from
time to time we will be rejected by people is something we
cannot change. That is inevitable in this fallen world. However,
the way we respond to these hurts is our responsibility. We can
at least seek, with the help of the Holy Spirit, to recognize what
needs changing in our behavior and to understand why we
behave in the way we do.

Here, perhaps, is the starting point for many of us. If we
are willing to recognize where our behavior, growing out of
these inner lies planted by past rejection, is leading us into sin
(remember what Elihu said to Job: "Take heed, do not turn
to iniquity, For you have chosen this rather than affliction" –
Job 36:21), we can perhaps bring some light into our condition.
Bringing more of our life into line with godly ways, through
repentance of our sin, is what John the Baptist preached.

> *Therefore bear fruits worthy of repentance ...*
>
> (Luke 3:8)

He told people to change their behavior in preparation for the
coming salvation. He had come to prepare the way for the
Lord, the One who is our Savior and Healer:

> *The voice of one crying in the wilderness:*
> *"Prepare the way of the Lord;*
> *Make His paths straight."*   (Luke 3:4)

He was talking about preparing the way physically for the Messiah on earth but also his words had another meaning.

We, too, need to prepare a spiritual path into the depths of our hearts, where the inner lies we have believed are rooted, so that the Lord is able to bring deep healing. When we come to Jesus in repentance of our wrong responses to today's situations of rejection, this prepares a spiritual pathway into our hearts for the Lord. By His Spirit, He will be able to come powerfully into our lives and will have access to bring truth into our innermost being. He can write over the lies with His truth.

> *... I will put My law in their minds, and write it on their hearts ...*
>
> (Jeremiah 31:33)

Nothing is impossible for Him. It is in our human spirit that those false beliefs have been embedded in our innermost being. Jesus will come and bring His healing to the pain of rejection, and establish His valuing and unconditional acceptance of us. His truth will bring freedom from rejection, so that we can be those who spread acceptance into the world, instead of more rejection. We can unconditionally accept others, out of the confidence that we are unconditionally accepted.

Fear of rejection leads to defensive behaviors

The past pain of rejection leaves us with one certainty: we want to avoid it in the future. For this reason, those who have suffered the sting of rejection tend to develop elaborate schemes for defending themselves. These defenses are largely unconscious, and seem natural for the given circumstances. However, what comes "naturally" comes from the carnal nature and, in the same way that Adam could not cover and protect himself with fig leaves (Genesis 3:7), so our attempts to protect ourselves from rejection are ineffective.

Fear of rejection is the driving force behind our defensive behaviors. Remember the man we spoke about earlier, who was constantly rejected in the playground by his peers, as unsuitable for their football team. It didn't take very long before he decided he didn't want to suffer that pain of humiliation and rejection anymore. He stopped trying to be a part of a team. He withdrew. He changed his playground friends and turned his back on the pain. By seeking to avoid the pain of rejection he placed himself apart from that group of boys, but this only served to reinforce his sense of rejection. Rejecting them didn't make him feel more accepted. He was in a no-win situation. He either continued to feel the daily pain of rejection or he withdrew and, turning his back on their rejection, denied himself what he most desired: their acceptance. As a result, he avoided all sporting activities and formulated some inner beliefs: "I'm not the sporty type" and "I'm not an adequate boy." These particular beliefs and the consequential thought patterns and behaviors affected his later life, and the repercussions affected not only his health and his sense of self-esteem, but also contributed to his concerns about his masculinity. Without realizing it, he had started to build his life on the sand of an inner belief that was not the truth.

There are many other faulty inner beliefs that are set up in the hearts of rejected people by the experiences of their past. They are hidden and often totally unrecognized, but they are the root stock of their present behaviors and thoughts, and need to be faced and brought to Jesus for transformation. There can be judgments about ourselves and our personal worth and value: "I am rubbish" or "I am useless" are common examples. There can be judgments about others, for instance "Everyone will always reject me" or "No one will ever take care of me." There will also be judgments about God, for example "God couldn't want to use me" or "God isn't interested in me."

Fear allows the enemy's authority

Probably one of the most common inner beliefs that comes out of past rejection is "I must avoid future rejection," and this is fuelled by the emotion of fear. Fear is a powerful motivator and has profound consequences on our lives. God says we should fear only Him, as fear puts us under the authority of that which we fear. When a person fears rejection it is as if they live under the power of rejection.

> For the thing I greatly feared has come upon me,
> And what I dreaded has happened to me.
>
> (Job 3:25)

Their fear draws further rejection to them. Satan delights in our fear. His kingdom of darkness is held together with fear. When we fear anything but God, we give Satan increased authority in our lives. The authority of Satan is maintained by unholy spirits. The chronic fear of rejection can allow a spiritual power to rule in us which seeks to keep us locked into future rejection.

This understanding will, I hope, stir you to anger. Life in the fallen world has wounded us with all kinds of rejections, and Satan wants it to stay that way forever! "Enough!" we should be saying. We need to allow this righteous anger to motivate us to earnestly seek God's way forward, so that we can truly leave behind this fear of rejection as the motivator of our behavior. The Scripture tells us that if we ask for wisdom it will not be denied us.

> If any of you lacks wisdom, let him ask of God, who gives to all liberally and without reproach, and it will be given to him.
>
> (James 1:5)

So, where did this fear of rejection start? Facing the root in reality will be an important part of our moving forward into freedom. The people who rejected us may or may not have meant to control us by making us afraid of the pain of their possible rejection. However, this was the inevitable effect. We became controlled by fear, even if they mistakenly thought it was a good way to discipline us and train us to be obedient. It is vital for any of us for whom this has been the case to recognize that, more often than not, those who have controlled us in this way did not realize they were sowing fear into our hearts. Sadly, we may well have used the same method in our own relationships with family or even so-called friends. In our insecurity, caused by the lack of assurance of our acceptability, we have perhaps tried to gain control and demand acceptance. Maybe we need to ask ourselves the question, "Have I used *others'* fear of *my* rejection as a control mechanism?"

After facing the reality of the wrong beliefs that are rooted in our past, we can start to think about forgiving those who have caused us to be gripped by this fear, whether they did it intentionally or not. The repentance for our own sin of using that same fear of rejection to control others will also be a necessary part of the healing process. We are then moving forward into a place to receive real healing from God and to find a true sense of His acceptance. In Chapter 11 we will discuss more fully how to pray about these issues. But fear of rejection is not the only problem that grows out of these inner lies.

Is it me or them?

When we are rejected we realize that something is wrong and endeavor to make some sense of why we are being rejected. We conclude, subconsciously, one of two possible theories.

The first possibility is that we embrace the lie, "I am the problem. I am not acceptable, and the person who rejected me is perfectly right to do that." We have already started to consider how this sense of unacceptability can affect and motivate behavior, in the last chapter. We will look further at how this belief affects us and our sense of identity, in future chapters.

The second possibility is, "The person who hurt me is wrong for rejecting me, so I will despise him and reject all his opinions of me." This way of interpreting the problem is the starting point for rebellion, a common behavior outworking from a root of rejection.

Rebellion – you are wrong!

Let us think more about rebellion: rebellion is refusing to conform or submit to a godly authority. You certainly don't have to look very far to see rebellion. We read about it in the newspaper, we see it on the television news, and we recognize it in our school classrooms. The world is full of rebellion because the world is full of rejection. The two have gone hand-in-hand since man sinned in the Garden of Eden. Rebellion is our way of saying to others, in a strong and aggressive manner, "I reject you and your values!" Someone once famously coined the phrase, "Attack is the best form of defense." Rebellion is a classic case: it is a defense against the pain of rejection. However, rebellion has a deathly sting in its tail. Rebellion has the effect of further alienating those who rebel, even if this is never acknowledged, which brings more pain of rejection and hence increases insecurity. Rebellion, rather than helping the rebel to feel better, makes matters far worse. It is a vicious and destructive cycle that, as we have seen in recent times, can end in an extreme form of rebellion: terrorism.

We may not be terrorists but many of us are rebellious. Let us consider our behavior honestly and, perhaps, a little more objectively. Do we push away authority figures, assuming they will try to control us? Do we refuse those who try to offer any hint of discipline or even good advice, convinced that we know what is best for us? Do we flout the law, driving at the speed of our choice, whatever the limit, because we want what suits us best? Do we blame others for causing our pain, and get angry about our needs not being met? These are the outworking of rebellion.

We all recognize that rebellion is sin, especially when others rebel against us, but perhaps we are slower to see how we engage in rebellion every day in a myriad of small ways. Rebellion is a sinful heart attitude. The heart is saying, "I am unsafe and likely to be rejected, unless I do things in the way I think is best for me." It seems as if trusting someone else and doing what they ask will increase my insecurity, so I rebel against their authority, accepting my own authority as best. We are trying to be our own means of acceptance, because under our own authority we can choose whom we accept. In this way, we believe we can accept ourselves, value ourselves, and boost our confidence and our significance. These things *are* what we need – remember that God gave us this need to be accepted, valued, and affirmed – but our God-given needs will never be satisfied in this way. Rebelling against godly authority is the same as rebelling against God. Sadly, because rebellion is sin, it will always bring more harm than good, even if it seems to bring a little temporary satisfaction. Rebellion may also bring further harsh responses from those in authority which will further the sense of rejection and reinforce the attitudes of rebellion. The cycle is complete and increasingly destructive.

Rejected, rebellious, and angry!

Rebellious people are angry people. Anger can fuel their determination and empower their rebellion. To some extent a person's anger may be justified. Somewhere, they have missed out on the life-giving unconditional acceptance that God intended for them. There may have been major issues of outright rejection through abandonment, betrayal, or just a lifetime of neglect and apathy. Some of the anger a rejected person feels comes from this deep wounding, and is righteous anger. God is angry about these situations too!

However, when we allow this righteous anger to fester in denial or to breed resentment and bitterness, it very quickly becomes tainted with unrighteous anger, which is generated when we don't get our own way, and in the way we want it. These issues can form another blockage to the healing we so desperately need for the wounds of rejection. Truth and reality about our behavior will be a necessary starting point. Honest repentance of our sin will prepare the way, so that with the enabling of the Holy Spirit we can effect the change that is necessary in our behavior. Jesus can and will help us to release the righteous anger in a safe way, once it has been recognized and owned, but the unrighteous anger needs to be brought to the cross in repentance.

The truth is that all rejected people are angry people, although our anger may be very well buried and under strong self-control. We bury our anger because it gives others another reason to reject us. We have learned that it makes us unacceptable. Many have concluded this as they grew up. I wonder how many of us were sent to our bedroom if we showed any sign of anger, and only allowed to return when we had changed our tone and suppressed our feelings. We learn that anger is not acceptable, and this may have been reinforced by wrong teaching about anger in the Church. Contrary to what some Christians seem to believe, anger is not always sin (Ephesians 4:26). Jesus Himself expressed His anger on more than one occasion, but He never sinned (Hebrews 4:15).

Angry people sometimes feel that if their anger is not expressed it might go away, or at least remain unrecognized. However, this is not the case. Colleagues, family, and friends will be able to give testimony to the pressure that they can feel within a person who is harboring deep wounds of rejection, even if the anger is never allowed to explode. Angry, rejected people are driven people. This driven-ness may be seen as determination and may even be welcomed as a great asset in the business world, but it is definitely not the way to find peace and to have a happy, long, fulfilled, and healthy life.

Judging makes me feel superior!

Rebellious people are often judgmental and critical of others. They are usually working on an unconscious premise that if you expose the weaknesses of others, you will feel better about yourself. However, nothing could be further from the truth. The critical person is usually inwardly only too aware of their own shortcomings, and is secretly very self-critical and despising of their own weaknesses. There are nagging doubts about their own worth and acceptability. The judgmental attitude is a defense which is actively trying to override their sense of unacceptability so that it will remain unnoticed to those around them. Perhaps they are even trying to deny the truth to themselves! They may gradually move into self-deception, boasting about their supposed accomplishments, sometimes to the point of obvious unreality.

Self-deception is a very slippery path. The rebellious person starts by becoming their own authority in their behavior and lifestyle. The end of the path is that they cut themselves off from all accountability to any higher authority. They become their own higher authority; that is, they become their own god. Paul warns that if we stray from desiring the lordship of Jesus and His truth, then, eventually, delusion will ensue and bring destruction.

> *… because they did not receive the love of the truth, that they might be saved. And for this reason God will send them strong delusion, that they should believe the lie.*

> (2 Thessalonians 2:10–11)

The lie which they believe is that it is safer to reject everyone's wisdom except their own. They deduce that this will make them feel safer and more valuable, but of course this is only in their own fallen estimation. The real consequence is that they are locked into their own world of delusion, and no one can help them to unlock the door – ultimately, maybe not even Jesus.

In the next chapter, we will consider the outworking of the other inner belief that may have been formed as a result of trying to make sense of early rejections: the belief, "I am the one who is rubbish, and everyone else is right to reject me." This belief has settled deep in the spirit of many people who know they need healing from rejection. This inner judgment against ourselves germinates and can potentially grow into a chronic lifelong problem. Whatever we choose to call it – self-consciousness, low self-esteem, lack of self-worth, self-denigration – it is, in truth, self-rejection.

CHAPTER 8

Accepting Yourself – Who Makes the Grade?

A sickness that destroys potential

There is a pandemic, it seems, that is prevalent in the world today. It infects us with a life-limiting infection. It spreads like a disease carried by germs, but this is a spiritual disease and these are spiritual germs. They are germs of ideas that infect the inner thoughts through words, pictures, and relationships. It is an illness that affects our innermost being, and the initial symptoms are not immediately apparent to others. They are hidden, but are nonetheless dangerous to our well-being. Whether we think we are affected or not, we all seem to succumb to an outbreak of this disease from time to time. Some have suffered chronically since their childhood and it may reach an acute stage in the teen years. This illness, if untreated, can lead to death. It is the life-limiting disease of *self-rejection*.

Sufferers exist with a joyless and impoverished life, for there is little or no hope of abundant life while suffering from this disease. Everyone knows that agreeing with God is a good idea, since He is eternally right, yet those who live with self-rejection are not able to agree with God about a most crucial issue: their value and worth. The psalmist makes it plain how God wants us to see ourselves.

I will praise You, for I am fearfully and wonderfully made;
Marvelous are Your works,
And that my soul knows very well.

(Psalm 139:14)

Most Christians are very familiar with this verse and would *like* to be able to agree with it wholeheartedly. We want to see ourselves as "fearfully and wonderfully made" but many just cannot embrace the truth of this verse for themselves.

Somehow this truth seems untrue for them. The bottom line is that having received and incubated germs of self-rejection, the negative beliefs and feelings about themselves have become firmly entrenched and have freely multiplied. The validity of these feelings seems beyond question, and it therefore seems impossible that it could ever be any different. Having been infected with this disease is certainly bad news, but being willing to go on suffering with the disease is foolishness and unnecessary. *There is a cure!*

For those who are willing to face the pain for the sake of the gain, Jesus has the healing power that is necessary. It takes energy to fight off this chronic illness but, with good care and loving support, anyone who desires it can be fully restored to a healthy life – a life lived in the certain knowledge of the absolute, God-confirmed truth that you are an unconditionally accepted and valued child of the King, with a purpose and a destiny.

Catching the disease

So, why are so many people in this sick state, suffering from self-rejection? There are many and various reasons why people are exposed to the "germs" that cause this diseased inner belief of unacceptability. We have already touched on some of these in earlier chapters. We have mentioned that those who have suffered rejection will try to make sense of their experiences, and we considered the beliefs that led to rebellious behavior. Now we need to look at the other possible belief system rising out of the past: that other people must be correct in their judgment and we must be, as they imply, unworthy of acceptance, worthless, and not up to standard. There is a paradox here. When we agree with others, it can bring some small sense of security because we belong to a like-minded group and this brings a modicum of acceptance. Perversely, the belief we are agreeing with is "I am not acceptable!" In reality, this is the point at which many people begin to be blighted by the disease, which continues to grow and to destroy their personal sense of worth and value. Once established and embraced as an identity, this self-rejecting belief is reinforced in a multitude of ways: we think negative thoughts about ourselves that feed it, we speak negative words about ourselves that enlarge it, and we neglect our own spiritual well-being, which gives it plenty of room to develop.

Self-rejection can begin to infect our lives from our earliest days as it can be an offshoot of all types of rejection. We have already recognized that even in the womb, long before we could understand any words that were being spoken, we were sensing the desires of our parents regarding us. If they wanted a boy but we intuitively knew in our human spirit that we were a girl, we sensed that we could not be what they wanted. We felt that we were a disappointment, and therefore felt rejected. Later, we may also have sensed their disappointment that we were not as quick to reach milestones of development as other people's children, or not as attractive or as appealing as they would have liked. We are made with an inbuilt desire to please our parents, and if they were less than delighted with us, we will naturally have felt the same about ourselves.

Many children are encouraged to compare themselves with others at every stage of their development and, inevitably, sometimes find themselves wanting. This practice may be an overt teaching or else it can be something that is just learned subliminally from the attitudes of parents and others in authority. Failings and weaknesses may be pointed out and, even in successes, there can often be a negative comment that steals from our sense of worth.

One young woman, whom I knew well, remembers the day she scored 98% in a mathematics examination. Her dad asked her, "What happened to the other 2%?" It could have been a joke but, sadly, it wasn't. Throughout her childhood, he constantly pointed out her deficiencies, personal weaknesses, and failures. This gave rise to a lifestyle of perfectionism. Her resulting driven nature led to academic success, but still she never felt good enough. More qualifications didn't seem to help her feel better about herself. She was always motivated by trying to be the best and she constantly strove to be above criticism. This led to her being considered very successful in her chosen career in marketing, and this success further fuelled her driven-ness but never really made her feel good enough. When the company lost a large contract that she was overseeing, she was overwhelmed with her sense of failure and, quite unexpectedly as far as her office colleagues were concerned, she tried to commit suicide. Self-rejection had been festering for all the years of her life, and finally showed its true nature as a potentially fatal disease.

Adverts and toys that spread the disease

However, it is not just the obvious issues of academic comparison that fuel the self-rejection problem. There are more subtle forces at work. We are surrounded by subliminal information about "acceptable norms." In every advertisement, film, and magazine there is an unspoken comment about what is acceptable. The acceptable size and shape for a catwalk model is, the industry openly admits, unobtainable unless the models starve themselves. Nevertheless, the fact that they "look good" in the high-fashion, expensive clothes makes them a role model for impressionable girls, and even mature women can be influenced. The fashion trade and clothing retailers feed the idea that a certain unnaturally small dress size is what is desirable for everyone, and we believe them. Slimming magazines remind us constantly that slimmer is better, and advertisements on the television seem constantly to point out that anything less than perfect is unacceptable. The message is clear: having wrinkles, grey hair, spots, irregular teeth, sagging waistline – in fact, whatever blemish you have – makes you unacceptable. No wonder self-rejection is able to take hold of lives so easily.

Very young girls may even be infected by seeds of self-rejection as they play with their dolls. The shape of a doll like "Barbie" is so distorted that it does not, in truth, reflect the shape of any normal adult female person. Yet it may subtly imply to the child that you must have long legs, a tiny waist, a big bust, and long blonde hair to be a beautiful and accepted woman. These attributes are impossible for a small girl with a flat chest and short legs. But the sense that she is not adequate in her childhood normality may be recorded in her subconscious mind, and gradually influence her life in destructive ways.

What is more, as far as the child is concerned, Barbie gets all she wants. She has a nice house, a handsome boyfriend (called Ken, in Barbie's case), and a pink sports car. Unrecognized and inaccurate connections are easily made by the little girl. To get these nice things and be successful with men, you need to look a certain way. The magazines and comics children look at, and the television programs and advertisements they see, can reinforce this belief. The daily influence of an ever-slimming or overly body-conscious mother may also add to this same image issue. Many a little girl subconsciously believes that she is not adequate as she is. Girls as young as five years old have been known to request cosmetic surgery in recent years. Such a little girl believes, "I must be different from how I am; I am not thin enough, pretty enough, or tall enough, so I must change to succeed – I am not good enough as I am." The disease of self-rejection is taking hold!

Who makes the standard?

But possibly, for you, it was not what people said about what you looked like that fuelled your self-rejection. Perhaps it was your lack of physical strength or sporting prowess that made others reject you, and in your embarrassment you just agreed with their verdict and so rejected yourself. Deeply rooted self-rejection affects our thoughts, our actions, and our hopes. Our embracing self-rejection allows it to become our identity and to steal our God-given potential and destiny. We aren't up to the mark, wherever the mark is! We are definitely beneath the standard required, full stop. This is the foundational belief of so many people – people who feel they are wrong, utterly wrong, because they look wrong, are unable to do things that others can do, have failed some social "norm," or just because they are who they are!

I wonder if we should stop and consider just who sets this unachievable standard, who defines where the "mark" for acceptability is. Perhaps a story would help us to consider this point.

One lunchtime a man was walking along a street in Amsterdam when, looking down, he saw a small grey stone lying on the pavement. He was just about to bend down to take a closer look when a boy came running by and kicked the stone, sending it spinning into the gutter. People hurried past, but the man bent down at the gutter and, searching carefully among the rubbish, he eventually found the grey pebble. Carefully, he picked it up and put it in his pocket as he hurried back to his office. He hung up his coat and began his work. With the tools of his trade he worked hard all that day and

on through the night. It was late the following evening before
he had finished his work. There, lying on a leather pad on the
table, was the result of his labors. Amazingly, now clear for
all to see, glistening and sparkling, it was a beautiful cut and
polished diamond.

Now let me ask you a question. Was the true worth of the
stone less, because others did not recognize its intrinsic value?
Surely, to the untrained eye it looked ordinary, useless even, but
its value was not about what unskilled people could see, but
what the master craftsman knew to be the truth. If others had
known what the man with the knowledge and wisdom knew,
they would have seen that stone very differently. The eyes of the
expert see differently. The man who knew all about diamonds
saw the potential and the truth about that stone. The moral
of this story is clear. Others may not see your true value but
there is One who does. He knows all about you and sees your
worth. He is an Expert in precious things. He has all available
knowledge, completely understands His creation, sees your
beauty and preciousness, and recognizes what others in their
ignorance do not see!

You may have been kicked into the gutter of life, but the
One who truly knows all things sees the "you" He planned
and intended for you to be. He earnestly desires that you also
recognize your true value and potential. He formed you to shine
brightly for Him like a diamond reflecting His light. Just as the
diamond-cutter had work to do to reveal the stone's potential
for others to see, so our loving Heavenly Diamond-Cutter may
need to work a little on us – cutting and polishing our lives to
be all we can be. Isn't that what Paul tried to explain to the first-
century Church?

> *But we all, with unveiled face, beholding as in a mirror the glory of the*
> *Lord, are being transformed into the same image from glory to glory, just*
> *as by the Spirit of the Lord.*

> (2 Corinthians 3:18)

We need to choose to believe what the Expert says about us and allow Him to work, so we can fulfill our true potential, shining for Him with God-given glory.

So, why do we allow ourselves to be influenced by the words and actions of those who are, by comparison, ignorant, and dismiss the knowledge of the Great Expert? The God who formed diamonds also formed you. Are you willing to believe this? We all know that diamonds are valuable because of their great beauty but, more especially, because of their rarity. But you are not just rare; you are absolutely unique. No one else has the same fingerprints; no one else has your abilities, your thoughts, or your voice. There is no one else like you. There are no two people who are exactly alike – even identical twins have some differences. You are more valuable than a rare painting, even a Rembrandt or a Monet! You are as unique as the Rosetta Stone! A priceless treasure, a unique masterpiece made by the Master Craftsman – no matter what your feelings tell you, that's the truth of what you are!

I will praise You, for I am fearfully and wonderfully made;
Marvelous are Your works,
And that my soul knows very well.
My frame was not hidden from You,
When I was made in secret,
And skillfully wrought in the lowest parts of the earth.

(Psalm 139:14–15)

Complications can make this disease deadly

If the disease of self-rejection is left unchecked it can escalate to self-hatred, self-abuse, or even self-destruction. If there is little or no sense of personal worth and value, it can seem immaterial if the mind or body is mistreated. Those who feel they have no personal worth can easily be led into smoking,

alcoholism, or illegal drug-taking. Some may allow themselves
to be abused, or may indulge in self-harming activities.
In addition they may use, or rather further misuse, their
devalued bodies in an attempt to get the sense of connection
and acceptance they desire through promiscuous sexual
relationships, or even prostitution.

The enemy of our souls will be only too ready to hold
us into any negative beliefs about ourselves. They form such
rich soil for the growth of destructive thinking, actions, and
lifestyles. The truth is that if our beliefs about ourselves are
not in agreement with God, they are sin. When we sin we
give authority to the enemy, and he will seek to hold this
foothold in our lives with demonic power. A lifestyle which
is founded on self-rejection – or, worse still, self-hatred – will
certainly open a person up to the possibility of invasion by
an unholy spirit. The unholy spirit will keep every area of
the person's life that is affected by self-rejection, under the
authority of the enemy. While the person continues in self-
rejecting beliefs, the demon has a right of abode, making it
even harder for the person to get free from the negative beliefs
they have embraced.

Now the person has another complication to their problem.
There is not just the wound of past rejection and the sin of the
subsequent self-rejecting attitudes and behaviors, but also a
demonic power from which they need deliverance. Jesus came
to set the captives free.

> *The Spirit of the LORD is upon Me,*
> *Because He has anointed Me*
> *To preach the gospel to the poor;*
> *He has sent Me to heal the brokenhearted,*
> *To proclaim liberty to the captives*
> *And recovery of sight to the blind,*
> *To set at liberty those who are oppressed.*

(Luke 4:18)

Satan hates those whom the Lord loves, and will do everything possible to keep them from hearing the truth that would set them free to enjoy their Father's love and unconditional acceptance. Thank God that Jesus came and won the victory over Satan so that anyone who wants to be free can be delivered from such a damaging situation.

But we still have to do our part in the fight since, on earth, we are all still engaged in a daily battle for the lordship of our lives. The battleground for this skirmish is our personal sense of worth and value. Perhaps we can think of it as an aggressive election campaign for the right to rule your life. God is for you and sees your value, but Satan is against you and tells you that you are worthless. You hold the all-important casting vote. So, which way are you going to vote?

CHAPTER 9
It Isn't Fair –
Who Cares About Me?

Doing what comes naturally

We have seen that the pain of the rejection we have suffered and our reactions to those wounds can form intertwining chains of bondage around us. We have realized we need to be released, healed, and comforted with our Father's great love for us. But is there anything else that might hold these chains? Because if there is something else acting as a sort of spiritual padlock, it will also need to be removed before God's freedom and healing can come. I believe, after years of ministering to those with rejection issues, that there is something else that holds these chains together, and will restrict us getting free. This unrecognized spiritual locking device is something we may have done quite unknowingly but will severely affect our ability to get free. A little story may help to set the scene.

One day our black Labrador dog, Ben, cut his paw on a sharp stone. It obviously hurt very much and he pathetically limped to his favorite spot in the kitchen to lick his wound. He clearly felt very sorry for himself! In a similar way, many of us have been "cut" by "a sharp stone" of rejection and, suffering with a painful wound, we have done something similar. Because it came naturally to us, just like Ben, we have withdrawn, "licked our wounds," and felt sorry for ourselves. Although this may have felt comforting for a short while, unfortunately it has had an unexpected longer-term consequence.

Let me tell you more about Ben. His continual worrying at his paw didn't allow the wound to heal but rather kept it open. He did what seemed good to him, but it wasn't at all helpful for his healing. So, eventually, we had to stop him doing what he wanted to do, and seek help so that he would leave the cut alone and the full healing could come. That's our problem too. Many of us have tried to deal with our deep wound of rejection by doing what seemed to come naturally. We have felt sorry for ourselves and allowed ourselves to indulge in feelings of resentment towards those who have rejected us. We have gone over these thoughts in our mind and effectively been "licking our wound" and keeping the damage of the rejection "open." What is more, the open wound has continued to hurt, so we have become very sensitive to anything that would cause us more pain, particularly anything that could be construed as more rejection. Even small issues have seemed like "salt in our wound." Now we take offense easily, and the continuing pain of the open wound feeds our resentment and anger, which can lead to bitter, unforgiving, and judgmental attitudes.

Who cares about me?

The result of this scenario is clear. We feel no one cares about our pain and we wonder why our wound never seems to heal. Even God doesn't seem to care. The problem is that we have become locked into our own self-comfort and self-pity, which keeps the wound open and can never bring the relief and healing that we so long for.

But "Who cares about me?" is a legitimate question. It is the expression of the God-given need for security and love.

God plants that question in each one of us, and plans that the answer will come from the daily expression of genuine love and care of our parents. In words and actions they would say, "We care for you; you are our treasure. We care very much and God does too." However, for many people this question has been left unanswered and eventually, in desperation, they have replied to themselves, because it seemed the only thing to do, "I will care about me."

An inner decision to rely solely on self to meet our own needs for love and security may seem safe, but it has a disastrous effect. It closes the door to God's love and comfort, and also shuts out the possibility of receiving the love and comfort of others. Loneliness reinforces the "Who cares about me?" feelings, and can easily fuel the inner feeling of resentment and jealousy of others who, it appears, have got what I have always craved. These attitudes, although perhaps understandable at one level, are in truth sinful, and further cut the person off from any sense of God's presence. A bitter and judgmental root can spring up, causing those around the hurting person to retreat further and, it seems, to reject them more. This reinforces their belief that they are indeed only fit for rejection. The whole process is cyclic and is triggered whenever another rejection comes their way. It becomes a downward spiral into hopelessness.

A diagram may be helpful to explain this idea. (See next page: follow the arrows round, starting from the top, to see how behavior follows beliefs and beliefs are reinforced by behavior.)

Reinforcing the erroneous beliefs

The experiences of our lives can easily reinforce our feeling that no one cares for us. It then becomes very easy to take offense at the smallest comment or gesture that we perceive is a sign of rejection. It is a miserable way to live; everything is taken

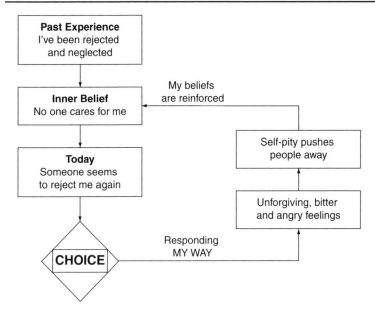

How beliefs get reinforced

as a very personal slight and it may seem to others that we are "desperate to be offended."

Imagine Bert, a person with rejection issues, walking down the street. Across the road he sees a man he knows from church, Patrick. He looks up hoping to be greeted, but Patrick walks on by. Now, Bert has a choice. Will he graciously assume that it was "just one of those things" and not allow it to affect him? Will he recognize that Patrick may have been having a bad day, forgive him, and turn to God for comfort? Or will he jump to the conclusion that he was being rejected, take offense, and refuse to forgive Patrick, because he feels hurt and angry? If Bert sees this as an incident of rejection and allows himself to take offense, then his expectations are confirmed and his beliefs about himself reinforced. Even if later he is told that Patrick had broken his spectacles and could not see any faces clearly without them, the damage to their relationship may already be done.

Taking offense is really holding a grudge against someone whom we have judged as having sinned against us. The truth may be that there was no real sin, but that we took offense because we see everything through rejection-tinted glasses. People took offense at the teaching of Jesus, although He never sinned.

> *... they were offended at Him.*
>
> (Matthew 13:57)

Taking offense implies that we are the judge of another person's actions and motives. The Bible says that knowing and judging the heart of someone is God's job, not ours, and Jesus tells us not to judge others.

> *Judge not, that you be not judged.*
>
> (Matthew 7:1)

When we judge we put ourselves in God's place... but we give no mercy! Taking offense is not an attitude of grace, but is the seemingly tasty bait that hides the hook of captivity to Satan. If you haven't read John Bevere's excellent book, *The Bait of Satan*, on this topic, I highly recommend it.

Offenses and grudges

For many years my husband David and I lived in the Highlands of Scotland. We noticed that there seemed to be a national sense of rejection felt by many Scots. This was probably brought about by the way the English, in particular, have treated the Scots historically, especially during the period known as the "Clearances." During this time, 200 years ago, a very large number of people were displaced from their croft land by the English landowners, to make way for a more valuable commodity – sheep! Perhaps this and other very real rejections were the beginning of a still prevalent mindset: an expectation of rejection. We noticed that, in the absence of God's grace, many held onto an unwillingness to forgive and had grown a defensive attitude which often caused them to take offense and hold a grudge. This seemed to have become, probably unknowingly, a miserably common way of life. It appeared to us that some Highlanders were still holding onto grudges after many years, and sometimes even when no one could actually remember what had really started the feud! However, the grudge and the offense lived on, and were holding many into a stalemate of bitterness where the past hurts could not be healed. Before we point the finger at others, perhaps we need to check our own hearts for grudges and places where we have taken offense in the past, and perhaps still do!

When we have set ourselves up as judge of others we have started to become our own authority, or in other words our own god. If we are our own god then we must provide what a god provides. The next step on this downward spiral that started with rejection is to become our own provider of comfort, love, acceptance, and sympathy. The drive to provide these things for ourselves leads to a totally self-focused life. All circumstances of our life are then perceived through a distorting lens: "How will this affect my life?" The carnal man will always try to decide for himself, first and foremost, what he thinks is "good" for him. That is the way of fallen man who has eaten of the knowledge of good and evil! Self-pity, sadly, is part of this self-focused life.

Self-pity leads to despair

Elijah had a bout of self-pity when he was escaping from Jezebel and felt he was all alone.

> ... he said, *"I have been very zealous for the* Lord *God of hosts ... I alone am left; and they seek to take my life."*   (1 Kings 19:10)

Job also suffered from self-pity and even wondered why he had been born (Job 3:11).

However, the Word of God tells us that it is not we who should pity ourselves, but that God is the One who pities us.

> *As a father pities his children,*
> *So the* LORD *pities those who fear Him.*

(Psalm 103:13)

The word "pity" in English sounds rather negative, and almost as if God sees our weakness and deems it pathetic. But investigating the meaning of the Hebrew word gives us a completely different viewpoint. The word translated "pity" really means "to love deeply, to show compassion, to tenderly regard someone." God wants each one of us to find this soothing and strengthening place of His comfort when we are rejected and left wondering "Who cares about me?" God says, in answer to our heart cry, "I care for you."

> *Blessed be the God and Father of our Lord Jesus Christ, the Father of mercies and God of all comfort, who comforts us in all our tribulation ...*
> (2 Corinthians 1:3–4a)

Instead of self-pity, we can find God's pity, which is sufficient to satisfy the very deepest longing to be acknowledged, affirmed, and cared for. We need to learn how to allow God's great love to touch the deepest place and bring a lasting solution to our needs.

The carnal nature takes control

When we embrace self-pity we are trying to meet our own needs. If we believe that no one else recognizes, cares, or is concerned about what we see as our impoverished condition, we can easily begin to feel sorry for ourselves and set about trying to meet our own needs. Our carnal nature, with which we all battle on this earth (Romans 7:14), is then given full license to take control, and becomes our god. A god is that which you serve in return for the provision of what you deem as necessary for your life. Now, Jesus says, you cannot serve two masters:

> *No servant can serve two masters; for either he will hate the one and love the other, or else he will be loyal to the one and despise the other ...*
>
> (Luke 16:13)

So, allowing the carnal nature to be master not only shuts the door to God the Father but also invites the enemy, the ruler of this fallen world, into the situation. A friend once said to me, "Don't throw yourself a pity party; demons come to pity parties!"

Self-pity is a dead-end alleyway. There is no healing to be had in this dark place.

However hard it is to recognize self-pity, it is crucial that we allow God to reveal it to us, if we have taken this route. Denial of the reality of our fallen and sinful state is so inviting to us, but recognizing our ungodly attitudes and behaviors is an essential part of the healing walk. This is where God wants to apply His life-releasing pardon. When we know we are forgiven we can be more open to the flow of God's healing, through the power of the Holy Spirit working in our lives, to bring soothing peace and acceptance. If our carnality is usurping the role of God Almighty, then what hope is there for receiving His covenanted loving-kindness that will meet the needs and heal the deepest wounds of rejection?

So next time, when we seem to be going down the spiral of self-pity, perhaps we should stop and reassess our old "automatic" reactions. The old ways haven't resulted in our receiving the healing for our wounds of rejection. Quite the opposite – they have locked us into our lonely, bitter, and self-pitying behaviors. Perhaps we need to consider making some new choices.

Take a moment to consider this new diagram below. I have added another arrow for the "choice" box. This is an alternative way of dealing with the issue when you feel rejected. Perhaps you can see how this different response will gradually change your inner beliefs, as you allow yourself to receive God's comfort for the pain. The old beliefs will be overwritten with God's truth – Alleluia!

Can you see how very different your life could be? Instead of reacting in the old way, and living in a downward spiral, you could make new choices and start living in an upward trend: a trend that would lead you into the deep knowledge of the truth of God's loving care, especially for you. The choice is yours!

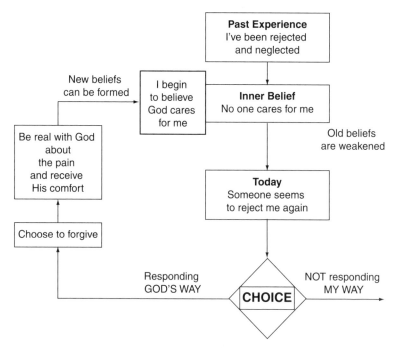

With God my beliefs can change

CHAPTER 10
The Search
for Identity –
Who Am I?

A question we need to face

In this world, in which so many people have failed to receive the
security of acceptance and personal affirmation, there seems
to be a recurring question: "Who am I?" The question may
never be formed exactly in those words, but it is a deep inner
conundrum of the heart. However, to be able to truly accept
myself and be at peace with myself, I desperately need to find
an answer – "Who am I?"

In the past, when running a nine-week training course, we
often asked the new delegates to introduce themselves on the
first evening. It was always very interesting to hear what they said.
Some defined themselves by their relationships: "I am Peter's wife
and I have three children." Some defined themselves by what they
did, or occasionally what they didn't do: "I am a doctor" or "I am
unemployed." Have you introduced yourself to someone in this
way too? These statements may be true but are not the answer to
this deep question, anymore than what I wear or how I behave is
the full answer. If all these aspects of my life were stripped away
I would still be "me" in some way, wouldn't I? We know that
physically we are a unique blend of the DNA of our two natural
parents, but is that it? Is there more to being "me" than this?

Body and spirit

The Scripture tells us that we are more than our DNA. We are not just a body, but a spiritual being within a body. In Genesis chapter 2 we are told how God formed Adam from the dust of the ground, and then breathed the life-giving human spirit into the form He had made.

> *And the* LORD *God formed man of the dust of the ground, and breathed into his nostrils the breath of life; and man became a living being.*

> (Genesis 2:7)

We are all made the same way, except that the "dust" for our bodies is from the egg and the sperm from our mother and father. These gametes together make a zygote, the first complete cell of a living being, which will then divide and eventually form a complete person – bones, nerves, muscles, and all. Scientists have discovered that a human body contains only substances that are naturally occurring in the earth.[1] It seems they agree we are made of dust. God's truth stands irrefutable for all time.

Our physical body starts to live when our human spirit enters this first cell. I have heard that when the process of fertilization is observed during IVF (*in vitro* fertilization) there is a measurable (although not observable with the human eye) flash of light. I'm not sure if this is true, but since God's creation starts with the bringing of light, as recorded in Genesis (Genesis 1:3), and Jesus is the Light that gives us life (John 1:3–4), it would not surprise me if this was so.

When God spoke to Jeremiah, He said,

> *Before I formed you in the womb I knew you ...*

> (Jeremiah 1:5)

Jeremiah had a special calling to be a prophet but he was a human being like you and me. This verse from Scripture tells us that God knew him before his body was formed. So it follows that God knew *you* before your body was formed. Psalm 139 confirms that this is true for each one of us.

> *My frame was not hidden from You,*
> *When I was made in secret,*
> *And skillfully wrought in the lowest parts of the earth.*
> *Your eyes saw my substance, being yet unformed,*
> *And in Your book they all were written,*
> *The days fashioned for me …*

(Psalm 139:15–16)

And not only did He know you but He formed you and chose you. Paul puts it like this in the letter to the Ephesians:

> *… He chose us in Him before the foundation of the world, that we should be holy and without blame before Him in love.*

(Ephesians 1:4)

It seems that God knew us and loved us a *very* long time ago! So, what part of each of us did God know? He knew the unique human spirit that He had put in each of us (Zechariah 12:1). He welcomed, accepted, and chose each one of us, individually, even before the start of our life.

My identity and my human spirit

So the beginning of the answer to our question, "Who am I?" is that, whoever I am, the truth of "me" is in my human spirit. The Scripture confirms this.

For what man knows the things of a man except the spirit of the man which is in him?

(1 Corinthians 2:11)

It is therefore in my human spirit that I can find the blueprint of the real person that God planned for me to be. It seems that the "real me" may need recognizing and liberating, so that I can accept myself and feel confident in my identity. Finding this truth will also lead to recognizing what God has planned for me – what we might describe as my "calling" or my "destiny."

For we are His workmanship, created in Christ Jesus for good works, which God prepared beforehand that we should walk in them.

(Ephesians 2:10)

He has planned things to give me a hope and a future that will satisfy and exactly fit my talents and abilities (Jeremiah 29:11). Wow! That sounds like a very abundant and joyful way to live life!

One word of warning is necessary. Some people try to find their "calling" in order to try to find their identity. That isn't God's plan. First we must discover our true identity and then our calling will exactly fit. When we find our God-given identity, the fullness of our unique personhood, we will also recognize our *true* desires. These will be desires growing from what God has planted in our hearts (Psalm 37:4). They will not be the desires that have formed and been motivated by desperately trying to be significant, striving to please others, or even by fear. God wants to give us the desires of our heart because He has put those true desires there, when He made us, both for our good and for His Kingdom purposes.

Spiritual wind

Perhaps a picture might be helpful to illustrate how our identity can become distorted. On the south coast of England is a place called Beachy Head. It is a high sea cliff where the wind blows almost constantly in one direction. All the trees on that headland are misshapen by this continual wind. They are stunted and leaning at the same unnatural angle, and are not displaying the correct form and shape for their tree type. They have the right conditions for growth: light, rain, and good soil, but the strong influence of a prevailing wind has proved harmful to their development and has distorted them. An arborist might have some challenges identifying these trees by their shape. He would need to look much more closely to see what type they are, since a large part of their identity has been distorted. It is true that these trees will never be able to regain their correct shape now they are mature, but we can rejoice that our Jesus is an able Restorer of misshapen lives.

Interestingly, the New Testament often speaks of wind to describe strong spiritual forces, both for good and evil. In Acts we read how a wind signified the baptism of the Holy Spirit that released the fearful disciples to be confident preachers of the gospel (Acts 2:2–4). Jesus rebukes a destructive wind in Mark's Gospel when it threatened His plans to demonstrate His identity and calling in the country of the Gadarenes (Matthew 8:26).

When a child is conceived, he enters into a spiritual, or to use our analogy we could say "windy", atmosphere. The wind may be a warm, gentle, accepting breeze and just right for good growth and development, but it can also be a distorting, chilly blast of rejection. This atmosphere will fail to provide the right environment to develop the truth and thus the right "shape" of the child's God-given identity and potential – just as has happened to the trees on Beachy Head. However, the balmy spiritual wind of affirmation and acknowledgment will release a child to develop, as God intended, into a confident person who has a real sense of who he is. Formed into his "right shape," he can fulfill his calling in the Body of Christ, whatever that may be. The truth is that the spiritual wind for many people is not this growth-encouraging wind but the life-stunting kind.

For those who suffer with identity issues, the root of their problem is often here. From their earliest beginnings in life, the significant adults around them have made decisions about what *they* require this child to be, and have given little or no thought to recognizing the child's God-given identity. So instead of God's plan for acknowledging, affirming, and accepting the little one for exactly who he is destined to be, he has received rejection of his true self and the pressure of other people's life-molding plans. A harmful spiritual wind, causing distortion of identity, has blown over him. The most important people in his life have dismissed, ignored, or even rubbished his true identity and, by enforcing their own expectations, desires, and purposes, have distorted what God originally purposed. They have generated a "wind," a powerful spiritual force that has stunted the growth and distorted the shape of the child's identity, not physically like the trees, but spiritually.

God's will or man's?

The problem is that the desires and plans of parents may seem sensible, even laudable. However, the lack of acknowledgment of the child's true identity is what causes the problem. Of course, children need to be disciplined, and their abilities and skills need to be rightly honed and developed. A child is not born with a fully matured identity anymore than a fully matured body, but all the potential of their true identity is there ready to be developed. The job of parents is to recognize this potential and, with God's help, to encourage its development to fullness. A secure child is one who is affirmed for who he is with his unique mix of talents and interests, whatever they are. A happy child is encouraged to make the best use of all his natural gifting, whilst also developing in his weaker areas, so as to become a rounded person.

One man, who had felt "lost" all his life, told me this story.

My parents were both teachers and I suppose they just expected us all to be clever too. My brother was OK at school, but I just wasn't the book type. I loved doing manual things with my granddad. He was really good at fixing things and encouraged me. When I was ten he died, and at the same time my dad really began to lean on me to do better at school. He made me take extra tutoring twice a week, but I struggled to get anything right.

Eventually, I did manage to do reasonably well in the exam and I went to the local grammar school, but I continued to struggle and, eventually, because my uncle was in the bank, I went into banking. All my life I have felt the same – trapped – and as if I don't have a purpose or any sense of satisfaction. My wife and I go to church, but I don't feel any great joy like others do. My wife says I have depression but, in reality, I've always felt a bit like this.

This man's problem was, at least in part, that he had never been released to explore and develop his natural desires and gifting, given to him by God. He had been molded by the preconceived ideas of his loving parents, who thought they knew what was best for him. Sadly, they missed the crucial point – he wasn't created to be the person they wanted him to be, to fit into their schemes and plans. He was created to be himself. Maybe they were concerned what others would say if he did a more practical job; probably they wanted their son to be upwardly mobile in a white-collar job; but, for whatever reason, they missed his real potential. Robbed of that true sense of identity with all its possibilities, the "real person" felt rejected. The true identity of this man had not been affirmed and accepted. He had been living his life in a spiritual wind that had distorted his true personhood, stunted his life, and stolen his *joie de vivre*.

Sadly, many people live in this atmosphere of rejection of their true identity. I am not suggesting that children should not be encouraged to develop all the skills necessary for life. On the contrary, if we are not instructed and disciplined we are not being rightly loved and cared for (Hebrews 12:7). But if those around us fail to see what we feel excited and passionate about, and fail to recognize and encourage our natural talents and gifts, then something of the "real us" dies inside and we lose something of our sense of solidity and reality. We can become a person living in an outwardly acceptable shell, like a suit of clothes that doesn't feel comfortable yet seems acceptable to the world. In short, we are living in a false identity. It is usually a gradual and mostly unconscious decision to adopt a false identity, but it seems to be what is necessary to be accepted.

Masks and gorilla suits

It comes very naturally to us to hide the truth of ourselves if we feel that we, or our lives, are not acceptable. We readily wear a man-made mask. A mask may be temporary: smiles at the church door when we don't feel very happy, extra politeness on the telephone when we are in an awful mood, or presenting an extra tidy house just for the visit of the in-laws. These small issues may not be exactly sinful and may be considered in our culture to be polite and good manners, but they are not exactly the whole truth. What is much more serious, however, is how we have perhaps been willing to compromise in the same way at a much deeper level. Our desperation to be acceptable may cause us to adopt a temporary mask for today's needs, but it may also have caused us, without our realizing it, to compromise the very truth of who we are. We might say we have been willing to "sell our soul" for the sake of acceptance, and to take on, not just a mask, but a whole suit of clothes that has covered and hidden the real person within.

We might think of this as wearing a fancy dress outfit, but one that has got so fixed in place that the person can't now get out of it. The costume is the image they want to project and it can be any image that seems to them to be acceptable to others. It may be the persona of a perfect, sweet, and charming lady; a macho adventurer like Indiana Jones; or even a scary big hairy gorilla! Whatever it is, the real person is stuck inside, hidden away and isolated! When we live in a false identity for much of our life, even one that has been forced upon us by others, we are living a deception and this is not in agreement with God, who is Truth. Life that is lived in such unreality brings us under the enemy's covering and authority, and his plan is to keep each one of us in the dark about our God-given identity and destiny. From under this false identity, we can never be truly accepted or feel we belong, because the real you, or me, is hidden and unseen. What we desire most, therefore, still eludes us.

There are many people who have, without knowing it, chosen to adopt and live in such a false identity. They have effectively rejected themselves. Consider the situation of a girl who has been sexually abused. The violation she has suffered will probably lead to her developing a complex system of defenses to try to protect herself from further abuse. But she may ultimately find refuge in adopting a false identity, one of "neutral" sexuality. She will probably continue to develop this identity that she believes, most likely subconsciously, will keep her safe. Her genderless identity will be expressed and reinforced through her thinking, speaking, attitudes, and choices, whilst her true identity becomes increasingly hidden. For instance, she might wear unisex clothes, avoid pretty jewelry, have a very short haircut, choose to take part in more masculine pursuits, and refuse to enter into activities associated with women. However, by doing this she is unwittingly negating part of her true God-given identity as a woman and therefore adding to the wounding of rejection she has already suffered through the original abuse.[2]

In these situations, in order for the person to receive full healing there will need to be a realization of, and repentance for, adopting a false identity. This will be as necessary as the need to forgive those who caused the original wounding that so affected their sense of personhood. Recognition of the depth of the damage done and a willingness to forgive are a vital part of the process of restoration of the human spirit, and the beginning of the answer to the question, "Who am I?" It is God alone who can bring healing and restoration to these deepest areas of damage.

Recognizing my God-given desires

Even when the past damage is exposed we may still be left with a problem. We may know who we are not, but still need to find the truth of who we are. To release ourselves into the freedom of the truth of our God-given identity, we need to ask the Holy Spirit to start to reveal our inner desires, so that we can truly know and accept ourselves as our Heavenly Father has made us to be.

We can start this process of revelation and self-acceptance by considering our own choices and passions. What situations excite us, or perhaps would excite us if we allowed ourselves to be part of them? I am not talking about constantly watching your favorite football or baseball team winning in the final, or continual retail therapy in the shopping mall, but when do you feel a real and lasting sense of satisfaction – of being like a square peg in a square hole? Is it when you do practical things? Is it when you are making order out of chaos, whether in the office, the home, or the garden shed? Is it when you are creating something absolutely new?

You can begin to recognize these feelings of satisfaction if you ask Holy Spirit to reveal them to you. Perhaps you could ask yourself, truthfully, "When have I felt this feeling recently?" and then be sure to *listen* to your heart's reply. There is no right answer. It is not what I think I should say that matters, but the truth of what my heart really says. It may take time for you to hear your heart cry, especially if you have been ignoring your true self for years, but it will come.

These inner desires need to be affirmed as God-given desires. It is not selfish to own them and embrace them; they are God's planting in you, so should be held as precious.

However, we may find we have another problem. Many of us have been infected with a lie – that what we enjoy doing can't be what God wants for us. We have been taught that what feels painful or tastes horrible must be good for us (especially so for cough medicine, I think!). The truth is that it *can* be a little uncomfortable, or even painful, to be straightened to the plumb line of God after years of growing crookedly. But things that do us good do not have to be painful, and things that God wants for us do not have to involve misery. What God intended for us He also made us to enjoy, because He has called us and equipped us with the desire to do these things. He planted in us the potential to grow into the fullness of His plans, in a way that would both meet the longings of our hearts and fulfill His will on earth. And when we truly move into this, we also enter into the delight of knowing and accepting ourselves, and enjoying the truth that we belong in His Kingdom. What a plan!

Becoming a rounded person

One word of warning is necessary. At the beginning of the chapter I mentioned those who define their identity through a "role." Some people might have easily answered my question about what satisfies them with a description of a "role:" "It is when I help people that I feel really satisfied," or "When I am teaching," or "When I am leading." These all sound very honorable and they may be part of God's plan for the outworking of gifts and talents of specific people. But an identity based exclusively on what I do (as a "helper," a "teacher," or a "leader"), even if this activity and gifting is part of my God-given calling, cannot be the truth of my whole identity. My God-given identity is not about what I do, but rather about the fullness of who I am, and remains the same even if my body or abilities change or fail.

The inadequacy of this one-dimensional identity can be revealed when, for example, the "helper" is no longer needed to help, able to help, or needs to receive help themselves. This may come about because of a change in personal circumstances or because the one that the person was helping no longer needs help. If this inability to be the "helper" evokes a sense of worthlessness and feelings of insecurity, then it is clear that the helping is not just an outworking of godly love for others, but has become something that has given a sense of identity. God knows and loves us, and since He is Truth, He will only heal and restore that which He made: the *true* person. It is therefore important for the person to face the truth that they have grasped an identity which may be founded on very real gifting and ability, but which they have allowed to become their total identity. The feeling, "If I am not a helper, I am nothing," exposes a lack of a sense of true personhood which has been hidden under a role or calling: a substitute for true identity. If it seems that the role of "helper" is the place of security and the only source of identity, then this truth needs to be exposed, faced, and repented of, before the person can grow into the fullness of their true self.

Some who have suffered from rejection, and are consequently unsure of who they are, turn to the role of helper because they desire to try to earn the acceptance they crave. The historic situation of lack of unconditional acceptance has bred low self-worth and a sense that others are more significant or worthy of having their needs met. We have seen how those who have been rejected as children, instead of valued and affirmed, will develop erroneous beliefs about their value, and even when they become Christians they often retain their inner beliefs about themselves. In fact, they may find a sort of encouragement in their wrong beliefs through specific scriptures which seem to endorse their thoughts, and which they take to mean that they are only fit for service to those who are more deserving (for example, 1 Corinthians 10:24). Of course I am not suggesting that we should not be servant-hearted, but it is the motive for our service that is important here.

Such people subconsciously deduce that by being those who give others help, putting the needs of others before their own and making themselves needed, they will be accepted. However, it is not uncommon for a deep resentment to build up when, despite their good deeds, they don't seem to receive back the love and acceptance that they crave to satisfy the inner desire for affirmation. The cruel twist is that the love and help that God intended would flow out of their inner being, to bring increased life to themselves and to others, has instead become a poison to their being and a hindrance to finding their true self. The "helper" identity therefore steals from the real person, and is clearly not God's intention.

One lady, a pastor's wife, told me her story:

I had got all of my sense of acceptance from being a "helper," running toddler groups, the church crèche, and various Bible studies. Then I fell ill with multiple sclerosis and became seriously disabled, so I was physically totally unable to do any of those things. It challenged my whole sense of worth. I had been a Christian a long time but I had to face the reality that I had never fully accepted that God loved me and valued me, just for myself. This realization led to a time of deep healing and gradual restoration of my true identity in Christ, not just a "helper" but His precious child!

The "helper" identity may well be maintained by demonic power. The reason for this is that the motive for giving help is not what it seems. The motive may at a conscious level be perceived as obeying Jesus' commandment to prefer and unconditionally accept others, but deeper down, it is tainted by a carnal desire to satisfy the helper's hunger for acceptance. In reality it is not an action that "gives" but one that, at least in part, seeks to "take." As such it will not bring life, peace, and joy to helper and helped, but rather distress and confusion.

A common identity among people with past wounds of rejection is that of a "rejected person." It is as if the person has given up the battle to find freedom from the past pain, and has agreed that they must accept this as their ongoing identity in life. They live in, and present themselves as, the embodiment of "rejection." It is their chosen persona. They don't have a sense that it could be different, and may find the possibility of change very threatening. We will talk more about how to move on from these wrong identities in the next chapter.

Loving myself is not narcissism

Many people who are suffering from the consequences of significant lack of acceptance in the past develop the idea that it is godly to negate and reject oneself. We all know that the Scripture urges us to offer ourselves as a living sacrifice (Romans 12:1), but a sacrifice of something that is not considered valuable is meaningless. So the truth is, we must value ourselves as God does and not negate and rubbish ourselves, if we want to be like Jesus. He knew His value and rightfully loved Himself. He was secure in His identity before He moved into His calling. His Father affirmed Him before He started His ministry, by saying:

> You are My Beloved Son; in You I am well pleased.
>
> (Luke 3:22)

The Scripture makes it plain: we must love ourselves *before* we can love our neighbor.

And the second [commandment] is like it: "You shall love your neighbor as yourself."

(Matthew 22:39, *emphasis added*)

How can we truly love, serve, and unconditionally accept our neighbor, if we do not even know and accept our true self? It is surely very bad news for our neighbor if, in reality deep inside, we have rejected our true self! We will then just be accepting them in a superficial way, to make us feel better about being obedient.

If I do not know who I really am, it is impossible to accept and love myself. If I think I am only the partial identity of "what I do," I will never have a sense of true love and value for "who I am." This means I can never really love my neighbor. Only when I accept my true self, whom God planned for me to be, will I be agreeing with God. Then I can be open to His love, and able to receive His all-satisfying, unconditional acceptance. His love meets the longing of my heart for acceptance and the security of belonging, and enables me to love others with the love that I myself have received. It cannot help but overflow to those around me.

Knowing and loving myself

"Who am I?" The question can only be answered by our Creator God, through the Holy Spirit who brings revelation of the truth of our human spirit. For rejected people, there may be numerous circumstances of their lives to consider. We might ask ourselves, "What was the prevailing spiritual wind in my early years, and how has this distorted my God-given personhood?" "What have I done to try to grasp an identity in an endeavor to feel more like a real person?" "Do I want to put down my firmly held beliefs about who I think I am, to discover God's truth about who He says I really am?" "Am I willing to put down my reliance on my calling as my only identity, and to let God show me the reality of my humanity – the person He made me to be, together with the wounds and sin that have marred my personhood?"

We have looked at many areas of our lives that may potentially have been affected by a dearth of unconditional acceptance in our formative years. In the next chapter we will look at some of the prayers we might need to consider praying to begin the reclamation of our lives. We now have some understanding and that is a wonderful start, but actively bringing all the negative influences we have experienced into the light and truth of the Kingdom of God is what will enable God's amazing healing to flow. We can do this by being real about what has happened to us and choosing to forgive those who have hurt us. We will also need to repent of our own sin which has followed on from our wounding. The following thoughts on how to pray will give you the next steps in moving forward out of the darkness of rejection into the glorious light of God's unconditional acceptance and the security of true belonging.

Notes

1. H.A. Harper, V.W. Rodwell, P.A. Mayes, *Review of Physiological Chemistry*, 16th ed. (Lange Medical Publications, Los Altos, California, 1977).

    Man is made of: Oxygen (65%), Carbon (18%), Hydrogen (10%), Nitrogen (3%), Calcium (1.5%), Phosphorus (1.0%), Potassium (0.35%), Sulfur (0.25%), Sodium (0.15%), Magnesium (0.05%), and Copper, Zinc, Selenium, Molybdenum, Fluorine, Chlorine, Iodine, Manganese, Cobalt, Iron (0.70%). Also Lithium, Strontium, Aluminum, Silicon, Lead, Vanadium, Arsenic, Bromine (trace amounts).

2. To understand more about how these issues may deeply affect someone's life, the reader might be interested to read *Sarah* by Sarah Shaw (Sovereign World, 2009); ISBN 978 1 85240 511 3.

The Walk Forward –
Will You Choose
New Truths or Old?

Change is coming!

Jesus declared that He had come to put to rights all the wrongs that mankind had suffered through sin and the consequences of the Fall.

... He has sent Me to heal the brokenhearted,
To proclaim liberty to the captives
And recovery of sight to the blind,
To set at liberty those who are oppressed.

(Luke 4:18)

And there is something else that we can be confident about. Nothing is too difficult for Him; however, He will not force His healing on us. The wonderful truth in the Word of God is that when we cooperate with God all things are possible (Matthew 19:26).

We have been investigating how we may have been wounded by rejection from our very first moments of life. The motives, attitudes, words, and even actions of significant people around us have been very damaging to many of us. We have recognized that some of our families have passed on an inheritance of rejection issues to us, and that we have learned from those around us how to try to defend and cope with the issue of rejection. We have seen how the atmosphere of our early years often brings a lack of affirmation for our true identity, and how we have been crushed by the situations that have rejected our true personhood. We have become aware of how self-rejection, fear of rejection, and rebellion can be maintained and empowered by the enemy, and that we need the authority and power of Jesus to deliver us from these spiritual bondages. But there is still one extremely important issue to face. Do you really want to move on from your old identity of rejection?

Over many years, people have been coming to Ellel Ministries to ask for help to deal with their past rejection. Many are delighted to receive a deep sense of God's love, and make wonderful progress that changes their lives. However, there are others who seem to go round and round the old issues, and somehow their rejection issues never seem to be resolved. Of course, there may be many areas that need specific prayer but, eventually, for some people it comes down to a very clear choice: do they want to move on from the old identity of a "rejected person" and become a new creation, an accepted person – or not?

Courage to step out of the comfort zone

It can be hard to step out of an old lifestyle and identity. The way your life is now is what you know, and it feels familiar. It is amazing how easy it is to feel sufficiently comfortable, even in an uncomfortable place, not to want to make a change. I remember a time when I was camping and I suffered all night feeling cold, but not quite cold enough to make me do something about it. I was not quite uncomfortable enough to rectify the situation by getting out of the sleeping bag, putting on another layer of clothes, and getting back into the bed. I would have had a much better sleep, but I didn't want the discomfort of the process of change.

Bartimaeus had to make a choice when he decided to call out to Jesus for His healing (Mark 10:46–52). He had a way of life that was relatively settled and was his "normal." He was a beggar at the city gate of Jericho, probably one of a group of official beggars. True, he was beholden to others for his daily bread, but it was what he had known for perhaps most, if not all, of his life. Even in difficult situations it is human nature to seek for an anchor of some sort, a routine, a usual way of "doing life," a "norm." So, undoubtedly, for many years this lifestyle had given him a sort of security when so much else was beyond the scope of his experience. But Bartimaeus was not willing to settle for his limited life. He wanted more. He was not satisfied to continue to be comfortable in this uncomfortable place, however much it held an odd sense of belonging. The Scripture tells us that when Jesus stopped nearby, he "threw off his cloak, jumped up, and came to Jesus" (Mark 10:50 GNB). He was not willing to stay in the old wounded identity. He was determined and dynamic in putting away the old and going for the new!

Do you feel the same about your life? If you do, then today is a great day to start taking back the land of your life. We will need the help of our Savior and Healer, Jesus. He is the bringer of all truth. He will graciously hold up His mirror so that we can see our innermost beliefs as He sees them. He will, with great mercy and love, convict us of our behaviors that are motivated by rejection. Nothing is hidden from Him. He knows it all already. The issue is whether you are ready to face what is necessary and allow Him to bring change. Someone once said, "Change is spelt R-I-S-K-Y" and I think we can all understand what he meant.

Jesus, alone, can heal our wounds and bring soothing comfort to the pains caused by rejection. He alone can forgive our sins: the sin of refusing to believe that the love of my

Heavenly Father is available for me, the sin of rejecting and
hating myself, and the sin of rejecting, judging, and criticizing
others. He, alone, is our Deliverer from the oppression of the
evil one.

Getting down to business with God

Some suggestions on how to pray might be helpful. Prayer is
the way we open our hearts to God. When we seek His will
and pray in agreement with Him and His will for our lives,
past and present, we step more fully into the Kingdom of
God and its power. Prayer opens the door that allows God's
miracle-working power to flow. But prayer isn't of itself the
fullness of that healing. Consider if you are physically ill –
you may need to take medicine. But it is no good recognizing
you are sick, being offered the medicine, and refusing to take
it. Neither is it any good opening your mouth to receive the
specified dose, and then refusing to swallow it. The medicine
can only work if it is ingested as recommended and allowed
to do what it is intended to do in the unseen places inside.
It is much the same with God's divine healing. If prayer is
opening our hearts to receive God's truth and love, which is
the divine medicine, then there is still a need to internalize
the "medicine" so that it can work in the hidden places of
our hearts.

If you are serious about rejecting rejection, then there will
need to be some "swallowing" of God's truths and healing;
that will be your part – no one else can do that for you. But
to open the "mouth" of your heart, perhaps you could make
a time to speak out the prayers that are outlined later in this
chapter, preferably with a Christian friend as a witness who
will stand in agreement with you. Speaking out will help you
to put more determination into the prayer. Remember, you can
use your own words in the prayers; what is suggested is just an

example for you to get an idea of how you might want to pray. Your words don't need to be clever, slick, or formed with perfect grammar, but to be effective they do need your willingness to be open to change. Remember, heartfelt prayers open your heart to receive a "dose" of divine medicine.

But then, with the help of God's Holy Spirit, *you* must allow *yourself* to swallow the medicine of God's love, which will work the necessary healing from the past wounding. You could do this by asking God to speak to you specifically after each prayer, and letting His truth go deep into your heart. For instance, after forgiving others for their rejection of you, when you perhaps may be feeling the pain of the wounds, you could meditate on what *God* says about your *acceptability to Him*. These words of life from The Word Himself are the medicine that puts right the distortions of the past, and feeds in the truth that was missing.

So, here are the prayers. There are spaces in some of the prayers for you to add the specific names, issues, or circumstances that you need to bring before the Lord. The prayers are not intended to be rushed. My suggestion is that they are used one at a time, slowly, and that you allow God's personal response to you to be the medicine of life for your healing. You might even want to spread the process over a period of a few days so that each prayer and God's answer to it can, in turn, receive your full attention.

Possible prayer for forgiveness of those who have rejected me

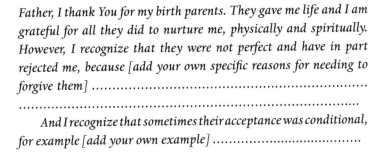

Father, I thank You for my birth parents. They gave me life and I am grateful for all they did to nurture me, physically and spiritually. However, I recognize that they were not perfect and have in part rejected me, because [add your own specific reasons for needing to forgive them] ....

...

And I recognize that sometimes their acceptance was conditional, for example [add your own example] ....

*I recognize that there were other significant people [name them]
.... who also rejected me by [add example] ....
....
    I now choose to forgive all these people who have sown into my
life the lie that I am not unconditionally acceptable just for who I
am. I release these people into the freedom of my forgiveness.
Amen*

Now take a moment to wait on Jesus for Him to tell you how
much He wanted and accepted you in the past and that He
accepts you, wants you, and values you right now, today. You
could speak out any scriptures that come to your mind that
declare this truth, or look up and read aloud one or more of the
suggestions below. Allow these truths to sink into your inner
being, and choose to let them work their transformation and
healing in your heart.

Isaiah 43:1–2; Isaiah 43:7; Zephaniah 3:17

**Possible prayer for release from generational inheritance
of rejection**

*Father, I thank You for my ancestors and for all the blessings that
have come down the family line into my life, because of right attitudes of acceptance toward You, themselves, and others. However,
I recognize that my ancestors were fallen people, as all people are,
and that they may also have sinned by allowing rejection to rule in
their lives. Lord Jesus, I understand that Your Word says that their
sins have caused distortion in my life and that this brings curses,
not blessings.*

    *I choose to forgive my ancestors for the negative spiritual effects
that their sins of rejecting You, themselves, or other people have had
on me; and I ask You, Lord Jesus, to release me from this negative
effect, and to deliver me of every demonic power that would want
me to be held into this family inheritance.*

Thank you, Jesus, that I have been adopted into Your family, in which I can receive the full inheritance of Your unconditional acceptance.

Amen

Now take a moment to wait on Jesus to speak to you about your place in His family. Again speak out any relevant scripture or encouraging words from God that come into your mind, or look up and read out one or more of the scriptures suggested below.

John 1:12; Romans 8:14–17; 1 John 3:1–2; 1 John 4:4

Possible prayer to forgive those who have trained me to expect rejection and taught me sinful ways to respond to rejection

Father, I forgive those who have taught me, knowingly or unknowingly, by their words or actions, to expect rejection. I know that fallen people will sometimes reject me, but I want to learn to change my expectations and learn to trust people more, creating an atmosphere in which people will find it easier to accept me and in which I will be able to receive their acceptance.

Father, I forgive those [name them] .... whose lifestyle modeled ungodly ways of response to rejection, especially .... [e.g. revenge, bitterness or self-pity]. Their behavior has impacted my life in many subtle ways, and I ask You to show me, by Your Holy Spirit, how I have followed in their ways over issues of rejection.

Amen

Now take a moment to consider how Jesus responded to rejection (Luke 23:34). Ask God to talk to you about how He wants to re-parent your life, so that you can change your thinking and learn to respond to past, present, and future rejection in a more godly way.

Possible prayer to repent of my own ungodly responses
to rejection

> *Father, I need to be honest about how I have reacted to feelings of
> rejection in the past. I ask You to show me the reality of my sinful-
> ness which, even though it came out of my pain, was still sin. I
> realize this sin has caused me more pain and has brought further
> separation from You and Your love. I now repent of my own sin-
> ful reactions and responses when I have felt rejected, both for the
> times when I have truly been rejected, and for the times when I
> simply perceived rejection [mention what you have done that is
> sinful]* ....

You may want to say the prayer specifically with regard to
embracing self-pity if that has been an issue for you.

> *I am truly sorry that I have chosen a sinful way instead of Your
> Kingdom way.*
>
> *Please forgive me and cleanse me from what has been my habit
> until today. I take responsibility for my past sin and ask You to show
> me how to respond differently. I realize that this will not be easy at
> first, but I thank You that You are with me in this, and that by the
> power of Your Holy Spirit, You will enable me. Please help me to
> look to You when I am tempted to respond in my old ways.*
> *Amen*

Spend some time allowing the Holy Spirit to convict you of
your past sinful habits, and then receiving God's pardon for
each of the ways you have tried to comfort and defend yourself
when you have felt the sting of rejection. You might want to
look up the following scriptures and meditate on them.

Job 36:21; Proverbs 16:7; Isaiah 1:18–19; 1 John 1:9

You might also like to read some of the scriptures below and consider some of the examples of godly responses to rejection in the lives of real people documented there. You may not be successful in catching yourself *before* you react out of your old habits immediately. However, each time you do react wrongly, but recognize you have gone down the old path, you can repent and pray the prayer again. Eventually, with the help of the Holy Spirit, you will be able to stop yourself before you react, and begin to respond in a new way. You may like to look back at Chapter 9 and remind yourself how a different response could make a very significant change in your life.

Luke 6:27–36; Luke 23:26–34; Acts 7:54–60;
Romans 12:2

Possible prayer to repent of and be delivered from my self-rejection

> *Father, I recognize that I have agreed with what others have implied by their attitudes, words, and behavior toward me – that I am not unconditionally acceptable. This is not the truth and I choose to reject this lie today. Your Word says I am unconditionally acceptable to You even with my present issues. Today I choose to believe You because You are the One who created me and recognizes my true value and worth.*
>
> **Proclamation:** *I command any demonic power that has held me into self-rejection to go now in Jesus' Name.*
> *I accept into my human spirit the word of God that, through Jesus' death on the cross for me, I am worthy to be adopted into His family.*
> *Amen*

Now spend time asking God to bring to mind scriptures or His specific words that will speak of the great value He sees in you, and decide in your heart that this is how, with His help, you are going to work towards seeing yourself. The scriptures below may be helpful. Be careful not to push away affirming thoughts and words about yourself; this would be like spitting out the medicine!

Psalm 139:13–16; John 3:16; Romans 5:8;
Romans 8:15–16; Ephesians 2:10

Possible prayer to repent of and be delivered from rebellion
Let God convict you, by His Holy Spirit, of where you have followed your own thoughts rather than let God's ways direct your behaviors. The following scriptures may help you in this process of confession.

Proverbs 3:5–8; Proverbs 14:12; Jeremiah 6:16

Father, I confess that, out of feelings of rejection, I have let rebellion grow in my heart. I have become my own authority, thinking that I will be able to keep myself safe, and have refused to listen to what others, including those in godly authority over me, have said to try to help me. I have even been resistant to Your words of life and have held onto what I think is best for me. Please forgive me for this willfulness and self-centeredness, which has caused me to resist change and has allowed the enemy to lock me into a lifestyle of rebellion.

Proclamation: *I also speak to any demonic power which has locked me into rebellion and, in the Name of Jesus, tell you to leave me now. I am choosing a new way and I surrender to the Lordship of Jesus. Amen*

Now reaffirm that you want Jesus to be Lord over your life. The following scriptures may be helpful. You could speak out to Jesus, in your own words, that you are specifically asking Him to be Lord over your behavior.

Psalm 27:11–13; Psalm 91:1–2; Proverbs 14:26–27;
John 6:68; John 14:18

Possible prayer to repent of not having been unconditionally accepting of others

Father, I confess that I have been so preoccupied with my own feelings of rejection and trying to meet my own needs that I have not always accepted others as I should. I repent now of my treatment of other people. I repent of my conditional acceptance of people, and of using ungodly ways [e.g. withdrawal of love, manipulation, disapproval, anger ......] to try to make them meet my needs. I repent of my rejecting attitudes and behaviors toward others that have not shown them Your love and acceptance. I am truly sorry for my past ways of relating to others.

I ask, Lord, that You would refocus me so that I can be a channel of Your unconditional acceptance to others.

Amen

Think of some of the people whom you have struggled to accept. You might want to make a list of their names. Then you could ask God to help you see each of them as He sees them, and to give you a little taste of His great love for them. The following scriptures may help you, and perhaps you could ask Jesus to show you new ways to relate to these specific people, from today onwards. This would show your real desire to change. It may not be easily or immediately accomplished, but the Holy Spirit will help you if you are determined to make the change.

Luke 6:35; John 13:35; John 15:12; Romans 13:8;
Hebrews 12:12–15; 1 John 4:7–16

Possible prayer and declaration of deliverance from demonic
power that holds me in rejection and fear of rejection

> *Father, I recognize that I have been following the enemy's way by
> allowing my life to be governed by rejection and fear of rejection. I
> confess that I have lived like this and ask You to forgive me. Today I
> choose to turn away from an identity based on rejection and the life-
> constricting effect of fear of rejection.*

> **Proclamation:** *I choose to take my life out of the enemy's hold, and
> today I take away any rights he has by my repentance of sin and
> forgiveness of others. I now command every demonic power which
> has taken advantage of these issues to go in Jesus' Name.*
>
> *I desire that Jesus be Lord in all my life, that His truth should be
> my truth, and I invite the Holy Spirit to come and dwell more fully
> in me and to anchor me into the unconditional acceptance of my
> Heavenly Father's embrace.*
> *Amen*

Take some time to image yourself safely held in the arms of
your Heavenly Father. Maybe look at a picture of a child in his
or her father's arms, and then ask the Holy Spirit to allow you
to sense in your heart this new place of security and welcome.
If you have the song "I Have a Maker" by Tommy Walker[1] or
another worship song which speaks of your Heavenly Father's
love for you as His child, you might like to play this and allow
the words to sink deep into your heart. The scriptures below
may also be useful.

Isaiah 49:15–16; Romans 8:31; Ephesians 1:3–6;
1 John 4:18

Possible prayer for release from my identity of rejection

Father, I confess that I have become comfortable in the identity of a rejected person, but that this is not what You intended for me. I now repent of continuing in this false identity, and I choose to forgive myself for, albeit unknowingly, living in this unreality. I ask You to deliver me from the hold of the enemy over this deception.

Today I choose to take off the covering of that old identity [in the same way as Bartimaeus took off his cloak] and I ask You to reveal to me my true identity as Your loved and accepted child.

As I learn to agree with this truth about myself, please help me to know myself more fully: my likes and dislikes, my desires and dreams, my ideas and my gifting, and to feel more and more confident in who I am. I ask this in Jesus' Name.

Amen

These scriptures may be useful for you to ponder, and for reinforcing your decision to allow God to reveal the true you.

Psalm 139:1–6; Jeremiah 1:5; Ephesians 2:10

There may be other things you would like to pray about, but hopefully these prayers will give you some patterns to follow. Our Father in Heaven is delighted to hear our heartfelt prayers and to answer us.

Call to Me, and I will answer you, and show you great and mighty things, which you do not know.

(Jeremiah 33:3)

Expect to begin feeling different as God continues His healing work in you. Expect that things will change in your feelings and attitudes, and embrace that change. You will find that you are able to deal with rejecting situations in a new way in the coming days and weeks. Times when previously you might have gone into the hopeless feelings of rejection, self-rejection, or self-pity are now an opportunity to choose to respond differently. God is working His purposes out in your life and, if *you* are willing, He will not stop working until His work is complete.

> *Being confident of this very thing, that He who has begun a good work in you will complete it until the day of Jesus Christ.*

(Philippians 1:6)

It may seem a daunting challenge but you do not go alone. You have a Guide who knows every step of the way. It is an adventure of claiming your place in the Promised Land. This is your home in which you can feel totally secure and loved, unconditionally accepted and warmly welcomed, and in which you belong for all of eternity in your Father's arms.

Notes

1. Tommy Walker, "I Have a Maker" © 1996 WeMobile Music/Doulos Publishing.

   I have a maker
   He formed my heart
   Before even time began
   my life was in his hands

   He knows my name
   He knows my every thought
   He sees each tear that falls
   and hears me when I call

   I have a Father
   He calls me his own
   He'll never leave me
   no matter where I go

   He knows my name
   He knows my every thought
   He sees each tear that falls
   and hears me when I call
   He hears me when I call.

CHAPTER 12

Sowing and Reaping Acceptance – Anyone for a Lifestyle Change?

Your Kingdom come

When we pray in church, we very often say what is called the Lord's Prayer. When I say this prayer I find I am particularly aware of the words, "Your Kingdom come on earth as it is in heaven." This is a very relevant point for those of us working on rejection issues, since in heaven there is unconditional acceptance for everyone. So, when we pray this prayer, we are praying that we want this to be the reality of our lives on earth too. If heaven is to be seen and lived out as much as possible on earth, then we are all charged with doing our bit to make it happen.

We cannot shrink from this responsibility. We need to model the Kingdom of Heaven as much as possible in all our relationships on the earth. So, quite clearly, it is down to you and me to model God's unconditional acceptance to others. What a challenge for those of us who have struggled with the pain and hurt of past rejection, but what a wonderful privilege to be an agent of change for the future!

Before you start thinking that this is a very tall order – being asked to accept others when you barely feel accepted yourself – let me suggest a verse that will encourage you.

... for whatever a man sows, that he will also reap.

(Galatians 6:7–9)

If we sow according to the ways of the Kingdom of Heaven, we also reap according to Kingdom ways. That means we also benefit from our unconditional acceptance of others, because we are sowing godliness into the world. Even if the people around us don't seem to change, God will bless us for our choices and actions. It is a win-win situation. Others are blessed by our unconditional acceptance of them and we are, in turn, blessed by God. Surely this makes the effort very worthwhile, even if it is a huge challenge to our old ways of responding.

When God made us all different it was for His purpose. He chose it to be that way. He is so creative that He just delights in differences; think of all the different types of flowers or birds that He made. One type of anything just isn't His way. Together in all our amazing variety, we, the people God has created, show more of the whole picture of His character.

Accepting me, accepting you

So, why is it so hard to unconditionally accept others? The answer to this lies in our continued lack of confidence about our own acceptability. The less we feel secure and loved, the less we are able to feel comfortable with those who are different from us and perhaps may reject us. We will feel safer with people who are "just like me" and more likely to accept me: people of my gender, my culture, my age, who share my interests or my passions. Any or all of these requirements may form the limited group that we naturally find acceptable to us. But there are others we struggle to accept. Depending on your own age and experience of life, it may be the young who are "rebellious hooligans," those in authority who are "controlling dictators," or the old who are "past their sell-by date" and "useless." Because they are different and we don't understand them, we fear they will reject us, so we reject them first. We are suspicious and it does not come naturally to us to accept them. We may feel this way because of previous bad experiences with a certain type of person, and as a result, we have made judgments which have become bitter roots in our hearts. This is not God's way and He doesn't want it to be our way either.

Jesus told a parable about accepting those who are very different from us. It is called the Parable of the Good Samaritan (Luke 10:25–37), and is so well known that perhaps we miss the point of the story. The reality is that in the natural way, the Samaritan was the least likely person to stop and help the man who had been mugged. Think of it this way. A man is attacked in your high street and left for dead. Several smart-looking commuters walk past, assuming this ragged heap in the gutter is a tramp who is drunk. They don't want to help him because they judge he isn't worth it. They reason he doesn't meet their standards for acceptance. But a group of lads in baggy denims, with shaven heads and wearing football scarves, stop and help him up. They call the ambulance and make sure he is cared for before going on their way. They accepted him and put no conditions on that acceptance. That is God's way too. They had a choice and they chose to cross boundaries of natural prejudices and judgments, and unconditionally accepted the man. Just like the Samaritan, the lads probably knew what it was to be rejected. Disapproving looks from elderly shoppers, suspicion from passing police constables, anxious mothers with buggies crossing the road to avoid walking past them – these were the norms of their lives. Yet they chose not to do the same but to live in another way: the way of Jesus, who always accepted everyone unconditionally.

However, unconditional acceptance does not mean we need to accept bad behavior or have no appropriate boundaries. This would mean we were open to abuse and manipulation, and allowing ourselves to be used and abused does not help anyone. We need godly boundaries: boundaries that maintain our self-worth and value, whilst we also accept others unconditionally; that is, we see them and value them as God does. Each person is a God-created unique individual, and we all deserve to be valued as such. But we should also want the best for others. This means that, as well as offering them generous forgiveness for any wrong actions toward us, we may need to be willing to engage in godly confrontation, because their bad behavior is damaging to them (Matthew 18:15). Honesty with grace is part of unconditional acceptance. In reality this is a difficult balance to achieve, but it should be our aim. True love is willing to lovingly discipline those under our care, not to try to mold them to our desires but to help them to be conformed to the likeness of Jesus.

We have been looking at how we would like our lives to change. Certainly there are healing needs from the past for many of us. There have been deep wounds that need to be healed, and we have needed cleansing from our wrong ways of dealing with that old pain. But even as we are in the process of receiving precious cleansing and healing from the Lord Jesus, we can begin to be outward-looking and consider how we can be an agent for change for the future. Remember, God wants us to know first and foremost that we are valued and loved, but He also has a destiny for each of us: "good works, which [He] prepared beforehand" as we read in Ephesians (Ephesians 2:10). It isn't just about me; it is about God and His Kingdom on earth.

Choosing abundant life

It is a vital part of our own healing for us to make choices to accept others, especially those whom we have found it hard to accept in the past. We make the choice, and the Holy Spirit gives us the power from within to carry it out. It may only be the smallest thing at first: talking to someone whom you know you have rejected and ignored previously; doing a small act of kindness for someone who you have always felt has rejected you. It takes courage and determination to change old habits, but when we do things God's way we open our heart even wider to receive His healing and that much-longed-for sense of belonging.

Today is the first day of the rest of your life: a life full of potential. You have been, or are being, rescued from your past rejection, and each step forward is precious. I am not suggesting in any way that changing our old way of "doing life" will necessarily be easy, but the wonderful truth is that it is possible with God's help. He is rescuing you from the old rejections and teaching you to find a new place of security in His loving and accepting arms.

This future is now before you with both its opportunities and also, no doubt, some ongoing challenges. My prayer is that you will find the resolve and determination to say "No" to the past, with its old ways, and let God lead you into your inheritance: a life of abundance that Jesus has already won for you.

... I have come that they may have life, and that they may have it more abundantly.

(John 10:10)

Testimonies of Rescue

June's story

I grew up in a family that was dysfunctional (but none of us realized this – we thought we were normal and everyone else was different) and I never really learned to relate to people properly. Many things, including two violent attempted rapes, a breakdown in my early twenties, and years of psychiatric care contributed to my deepening sense of rejection, to the point of feeling separate from everyone and everything going on around me. I believed that I was unacceptable, unwanted, and unloved; no better than dirt in the gutter. My mind was inhabited by angry, irrational, and powerful thoughts that would drive me to the edge of suicide. At times my mind did not seem my own – it was a breeding ground for lies. I was locked into cycles of wrong beliefs, and vengeful and hateful thoughts; my emotions seemed to scream out of control and my heart felt full of pain and bitterness. I was an insomniac and a driven person, always striving to get some love and acceptance but always disappointed. I had become incapable of being a functioning member of society; I was isolated, helpless, and hopeless.

But I cried out to God and Jesus met me while I was unconscious in hospital, having tried to take my life. I had never experienced love like this: I knew Jesus lived and wanted a relationship with me. This revelation was a foundation stone for healing in my life. I began a journey of truth and grace: the truth of Jesus and the truth about what had really happened in my life. It meant facing the reality of what others had done to me, forgiving them, and facing the pain. Real progress in healing came when God began to show me how I had reacted to cope with my pain, the thoughts I had entertained in my mind, and the beliefs that had grown in my core. Only God could unpick all these, make sense of the damage, and restore me. In prayer I asked Jesus to help me recognize the triggers that threw me into a downward spiral of darkness and lies, and to expose the wrong beliefs deep inside. He gradually began revealing the lies, and the Holy Spirit turned on the light in my human spirit and began writing in His truth: truth to feast on in my mind and to practice living in. It was not a quick process but God kept working with me and in me to bring revelation, comfort, and truth.

I had been incapable of holding down a job; I had been socially ill at ease; I had lived in torment; and I had been told I would never leave hospital. But the Lord Jesus has done and is doing an amazing job in healing me. I am changed (and that is what other people notice); I can relax and enjoy being myself; I am doing a responsible job; I am in leadership in a Christian ministry; I am involved with helping other people; I do some teaching. Perhaps more than anything, I live life more fully than I ever thought possible and have friends to share it with.

Mo's story

It took a long time, with God's help, for me to realize I had actually been rejecting myself for most of my life. My belief system was that I was not valuable and so everywhere I went I needed a purpose, a reason for other people to include me and accept me. From my earliest memory I was always trying to help others – a good thing in itself – but my purpose for serving was a selfish one: I needed to be needed. I struggled with low self-worth and craved praise and acceptance.

I married at a young age because someone asked me and I believed, deep on the inside, that this would be my only chance at marriage. I was sure that no one else would ever ask me. Still trying to find self-worth through serving, I ended up being treated as a doormat by my husband, and believed that the problems in our marriage were totally my fault. Eventually my husband despised me and rejected me. The best he could say was "I don't hate you as I don't want you to die." Isaiah 54:6 sums up his rejection of me!

Going through separation, and then divorce, I sought God's help through prayer ministry. Gradually, over the last ten years, I have received inner healing from the Lord. I am discovering that God has made me intelligent, articulate, and talented. I now endeavor to dress in a more feminine way, no longer afraid of being noticed. Ongoing skin problems are gradually resolving and I am now able to look people in the eye as a pronounced squint is hardly noticeable anymore. My praise and thanks to my Lord and Savior for all the true friends He has sent along the way! I am able to accept myself more and more, as I agree with God that I am "fearfully and wonderfully made" (Psalm 139:14).

Mary Lou's story

As an unborn baby, I knew the pain of rejection and abandonment because my father walked away. After I was born my mother gave me over for adoption as she thought this would give me a better life than she could. I was first taken into foster care, then put in a very large children's home. Finally I was adopted into a family. All this happened in the first three months of my life. Each time I made a bond with someone, I was taken from them. By the time I was in the security of a family, I had unknowingly made lots of subconscious decisions which would form the foundation of my life and my understanding of who I was. The result was that I could not trust, I felt I had no value or rights as a person, and above all I felt I should never have been born.

I lived with those beliefs every day of my life, but somehow around my birthday I used to get more depressed and angry. I desperately wanted to withdraw, and the words "Happy Birthday" seemed to stab at me rather than bring me delight and pleasure. In the days leading up to my birthday I was always filled with a sense of dread and on the actual day a sense of huge disappointment. Despite family and friends wanting to celebrate, I never could enter into a party mood and wanted to be left in my self-pity. As I got older, as much as I tried to enjoy and embrace my birthday, this deep sadness would come over me.

Then, a couple of years ago, I was due to spend my birthday all alone. It was likely to be an intolerably lonely day, but instead it was a day that was to start to break the hold of the damaging beliefs. Nothing very spectacular happened, but through very ordinary everyday things, like the sunrise, God showed me how important my birthday was to Him. It seemed, with each turn of that day, that I was met with the simplest of things which spoke of His love for me. It became very clear to me that although when I was born there was no earthly celebration, cards, balloons, flowers, pink teddies, or doting grandparents, my birth had been celebrated in heaven. I wondered what the sunrise was like on that day or how many flowers came out in bloom. And did the birds sing in celebration? I did not know the answer, but I did know that God, who created the heavens and the earth and had knit me together with such care, intricacy, and love in my mother's womb, knew all about me and planned my birth. It was with sadness that He had watched my earthly parents reject and hurt me; it was not part of His plan for my life. As things unfolded during that day, I realized that God wanted me to be with Him so He could restore all that I had missed.

This was just the beginnings of redeeming my birth. I had to walk the painful journey through the emotions I had felt as a baby and allow myself to cry the tears which I had never shed. The wound was very deep and very painful, almost untouchable, and yet as I cried, Jesus came in and began His healing. As He comforted me, I was able to forgive my mother and father and even call him my "dad" for the first time. I also needed to repent of the sin of choosing to live out of the belief that I should never have been born. I had made that decision as a baby but I was still living out of it as an adult. In that moment of repentance the power that it held was broken. The more I allowed the pain of rejection to be released, the more I was able to take hold of the truth that I am a child of God, fully accepted just because I am. I can now enjoy and celebrate my birthday each year and live in the newfound confidence of being accepted.

Annie's story

My parents were very young when they married, and I came along after one year. I remember sitting playing on the floor under the ironing board while Mother was ironing and she said, "Don't grow up and get married and have children like me, but have a career." I understood from this that somehow I was a blockage to her doing what she had wanted to do and I felt a sense of rejection.

My mother was a perfectionist and although she loved me, I could never fully please her. My grandfather remarked that she treated me like a doll and always wanted me to be perfect. I have come to realize that I had a core belief that she wasn't pleased with me because I was unworthy of love and not good enough to be loved. I believed that God loved me enough to save me from hell but was not sure He would want to heal me because I was not significant.

I developed multiple sclerosis (MS), which was aggressive, and soon I needed a wheelchair to get around. I desperately needed healing. As part of the healing process, I needed to confess my unbelief and accept the truth of God's love. I needed to receive a new deep understanding of His care for me in my inmost being. I received prayer over two years, resulting in much inner healing, but there was still no change to my physical condition.

One day my Heavenly Father brought some very special people to pray with me. I forgave my mother for her rejection and my difficult upbringing, in a deeper way than ever before. I also forgave her for leaving me so unprepared for raising a family. Curses were lifted and I was released from generational sickness and... I was completely healed in that moment.

The next day I chased my daughter around the local park – something I had never ever been able to do. I have now been healed for twenty-four years and have no further signs of MS.

About Ellel Ministries

Our Vision

Ellel Ministries is a non-denominational Christian Mission Organization with a vision to resource and equip the Church by welcoming people, teaching them about the Kingdom of God and healing those in need (Luke 9:11).

Our Mission

Our mission is to fulfill the above vision throughout the world, as God opens the doors, in accordance with the Great Commission of Jesus and the calling of the Church to proclaim the Kingdom of God by preaching the good news, healing the broken-hearted and setting the captives free. We are, therefore, committed to evangelism, healing, deliverance, discipleship and training. The particular scriptures on which our mission is founded are Isaiah 61:1–7; Matthew 28:18–20; Luke 9:1–2; 9:11; Ephesians 4:12; 2 Timothy 2:2.

Our Basis of Faith

God is a Trinity. God the Father loves all people. God the Son, Jesus Christ, is Savior and Healer, Lord and King. God the Holy Spirit indwells Christians and imparts the dynamic power by which they are enabled to continue Christ's ministry. The Bible is the divinely inspired authority in matters of faith, doctrine and conduct, and is the basis for teaching.

For more information

Please visit our website at www.ellelministries.org for full up-to-date information about the world-wide work of Ellel Ministries.

Ellel Ministries Centers

International Headquarters

Ellel Grange
Ellel, Lancaster LA2 0HN, UK
t: +44 (0) 1524 751651
f: +44 (0) 1524 751738
e: info.grange@ellelministries.org

Ellel Glyndley Manor
Stone Cross, Pevensey, E. Sussex
BN24 5BS, UK
t: +44 (0) 1323 440440
f: +44 (0) 1323 440877
e: info.glyndley@ellelministries.org

Ellel Pierrepont
Frensham, Farnham, Surrey
GU10 3DL, UK
t: +44 (0) 1252 794060
f: +44 (0) 1252 794039
e: info.pierrepont@ellelministries.org

Ellel Scotland
Blairmore House, Glass, Huntly,
Aberdeenshire AB54 4XH, Scotland
t: +44 (0) 1466 799102
f: +44 (0) 1466 700205
e: info.scotland@ellelministries.org

Ellel Ministries Northern Ireland
240 Rashee Road, Ballyclare, County
Antrim, BT39 9JQ, Northern Ireland
t: +44 (0) 28 9334 4401
e: info.northernireland@ellelministries.org

Ellel Ministries Africa
PO Box 39569, Faerie Glen 0043, Pretoria,
South Africa
t: +27 (0) 12 809 0031/1172
f: +27 12 809 1173
e: info.africa@ellelministries.org

Ellel Ministries Australia (Sydney)
Gilbulla, 710 Moreton Park Road,
Menangle, 2568, NSW, Australia
t: +61 (02) 4633 8102
f: +61 (02) 4633 8201
e: info.gilbulla@ellelministries.org

**Ellel Ministries Australia Headquarters
(Perth)**
Springhill, PO Box 609, Northam, WA,
6401, Australia
t: +61 (08) 9622 5568
f: +61 (08) 9622 5123
e: info.springhill@ellelministries.org

**Ellel Ministries Canada
Derbyshire Downs**
183 Hanna Rd., RR#2, Westport,
Ontario, K0G 1X0, Canada
t: +1 (613) 273 8700
e: info.ontario@ellelministries.org

Ellel Ministries Canada West
10-5918 5 St SE, Calgary, Alberta,
T2H 1L4, Canada
t: +1 (403) 238 2008
f: +1 (866) 246 5918
e: info.calgary@ellelministries.org

**Ellel Ministries France
(Fraternité Chrétienne)**
10 Avenue Jules Ferry, 38380 Saint
Laurent du Pont, France
t: +33 (0)4 56 99 42 663
e: info.france@ellelministries.org

Ellel Ministries Germany
Bahnhoffstr. 43-47, 72213 Altensteig,
Deutschland
w: http://www.ellelgermany.de
t: +49 (0) 7453 275 51
e: info.germany@ellelministries.org

Ellel Ministries Hungary
Veresegyház, PF17, 2112, Hungary
t/f: +36 28 362396
e: info.hungary@ellelministries.org

Ellel East Regional Nations
Veresegyház, PF17, 2112, Hungary
t: +36 28 362410
f: +36 28 362396
e: info.regionalnations@ellelministries.org

Ellel India
502, Orchid, Holy Cross Road, IC Colony,
Borivli West, Mumbai 400 103, India
mobile: +91 (0) 93 2224 5209
e: info.india@ellelministries.org

Ellel Ministries Malaysia
Lot 2, Ground and 1st Floor, Wisma
Leven Lorong Margosa 2, Luyang Phase
8, 88300 Kota Kinabalu, Sabah, Malaysia
t: +6088 270246
f: +6088 270280
e: info.malaysia@ellelministries.org

Ellel Ministries Netherlands
Wichmondseweg 19, 7223 LH Baak,
Netherlands
t: +31 575 441452
e: info.netherlands@ellelministries.org

Ellel Ministries New Zealand
info.newzealand@ellelministries.org

Ellel Ministries Norway
Stiftelsen Ellel Ministries Norge,
Hogstveien 2, 2006 Løvenstad, Norge
(Norway)
t: +47 67413150
e: info.norway@ellelministries.org

Ellel Ministries Singapore
Thomson Post Office, PO Box 204,
Singapore 915707
t: +65 6252 4234
f: +65 6252 3792
e: info.singapore@ellelministries.org

Ellel Ministries Sweden
Kvarnbackavägen 4 B, 711 92 Vedevåg,
Sweden
t: +46 581 93140
e: info.sweden@ellelministries.org

Ellel Ministries USA
1708 English Acres Drive, Lithia, Florida,
33547, USA
t: +1 (813) 737 4848
f: +1 (813) 737 9051
e: info.usa@ellelministries.org

*All details are correct at time of going
to press (September 2010) but are subject
to change.

About the Author

Denise Cross

Denise has been married to David for forty years and they have three grown-up children and seven grandchildren. Denise is the Director of Ellel Glyndley Manor which is the second oldest Ellel Center in the UK. She originally trained as a mathematics teacher but her life and the future of her whole family was radically changed by a "Damascus Road" experience of the Lord Jesus in 1981. For many years previously David and Denise had been attempting to live a self-sufficient life in the Highlands of Scotland but Jesus completely changed their views and focus and showed them how much they needed His sufficiency. Denise now delights to share her testimony and has discovered that God's amazing love and His dynamic truth transforms lives in wonderful ways. Her passion is to stir the hearts of believers to appropriate all the benefits of the abundant life that their Heavenly Father freely offers to each of His children.

The Truth & Freedom Series

Rescue from Rejection: Finding Security in God's Loving Acceptance
Denise Cross
£7.99 / 160pp

The Dangers of Alternative Ways to Healing: How to Avoid New Age Deceptions
David Cross & John Berry
£8.99 / 176pp

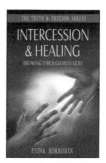

Intercession & Healing: Breaking Through with God
Fiona Horrobin
£7.99 / 176pp

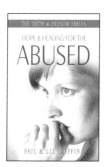

Hope & Healing for the Abused
Paul & Liz Griffin
£6.99 / 128pp

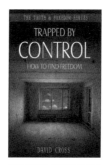

Trapped by Control: How To Find Freedom
David Cross
£6.99 / 112pp

Anger: How Do You Handle It?
Paul & Liz Griffin
£6.99 / 112pp

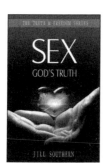

Sex: God's Truth
Jill Southern
£6.99 / 128pp

Soul Ties: The Unseen Bond in Relationships
David Cross
£6.99 / 128pp

God's Covering: A Place of Healing
David Cross
£7.99 / 192pp

Available from all good Christian bookshops.
For more information about these titles visit:

www.sovereignworld.com

Recommended Titles

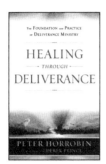

**Healing through
Deliverance (hardback)**
Peter Horrobin
£19.99 / 586pp

**Living the Life (FREE DVD)
Breaking through with God**
Peter Horrobin
£9.99 / 224pp

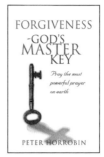

**Forgiveness –
God's Master Key**
Peter Horrobin
£6.99 / 112pp

Reclaiming the Ground
Ken Hepworth
£6.99 / 128pp

Pills for the Soul?
Dieter Mulitze
£11.99 / 320pp

Releasing Heaven on Earth
Alistair Petrie
£9.99 / 272pp

Sarah
Sarah Shaw
£8.99 / 176pp

**Frida: A miraculous escape
from the Rwandan genocide**
Frida Gashumba
£8.99 / 176pp

In Rebel Hands
Trish Perkins
£12.99 / 416pp

**Available from all good Christian bookshops.
For more information about these titles visit:**

www.sovereignworld.com